Sources of Religious Worship

BOOKS BY BASTIAAN BAAN

The Chymical Wedding of Christian Rosenkreutz:
A Commentary on a Christian Path of Initiation

Lord of the Elements:
Interweaving Christianity and Nature

Old and New Mysteries:
From Trials to Initiation

Sources of Christianity:
Peter, Paul and John

Sources of Religious Worship:
A History of Ritual from the Stone Age to the Present Day

Ways into Christian Meditation

Sources *of* Religious Worship

A History of Ritual from the Stone Age to the Present Day

BASTIAAN BAAN

Floris
Books

Translated by Philip Mees

First published in Dutch under the title *Bronnen van cultisch handelen: Van natuurreligie tot sacrament* by Christofoor Publishers, Zeist in 2010
First published in English by Floris Books in 2018

© 2010 Uitgeverij Christofoor, Zeist 2010
English translation © 2018 Floris Books

Unless otherwise indicated, Bible quotations are from the New Testament were taken from *The New Testament: A Version by Jon Madsen*, Floris Books 1994
Those from the Old Testament were taken from the Revised Standard Version.

MIX
Paper from responsible sources
FSC® C117931

British Library CIP Data available
ISBN 978-178250-513-6
Printed & bound by MBM Print SCS Ltd, Glasgow

Contents

Introduction

When one has practised a profession for more than a quarter of a century it is a good idea to ask oneself fundamental questions from time to time. Thus, after having been a priest for 26 years, I went back to the beginning with the following questions:

- How did ritual ever come into being?
- How did it develop up to our time today?
- Does ritual also have a future?

For any profession it makes sense to ask such questions about your own discipline, so that you don't lose sight of the essence of your work. The priesthood is a profession in which you work together with invisible, spiritual realities. In a society in which for many people reality consists exclusively of visible, tangible facts, you cannot afford to speak only in abstract, vague concepts.

In this book I am making an effort to connect my study of ritual with actual experiences at the altar. As in my previous publications, 'study' for me means not only exploring my own experiences and available professional literature, but also to try and make what I have worked through accessible in lectures and discussions.

Before writing this book I gave a series of thirteen lectures in the Christian Community in Zeist, Netherlands followed by discussions in which the intentions of this book were tested. The questions, experiences and critical remarks of the audience were helpful to me to make these complicated themes accessible.

In our time few people are trained to be conscious of ritual. This is not only due to the fact that ritual often has little relevance in people's lives today, but also because presently it is necessary to indicate concrete ways in which people can connect with the celebration of ritual. In our time it is no longer sufficient to say, 'Just go there, participate. It's good for you.' Especially in Chapter 10, 'The Senses in the Sacraments', I have made an effort to show a path of schooling in ritual. Sooner or later, such schooling leads to a heightened consciousness and stronger perception of what takes place at the altar.

Based on my own experience I can say that celebrating ritual acts may lead to a consciousness of spiritual reality that is more real than all visible reality. Once you have experienced this, words fail, because spiritual experiences are so hard to express. In spite of this, I am trying to do that in this book.

In the first five chapters I go back to the origin of different forms of ritual. I have been guided both by history, to the extent it exists in documented form, and by the spiritual traditions that tell us something about the origin. In Chapters 6 to 9 I follow the development of the Christian ritual, the Eucharist. The following four chapters are about specific ritual themes, and in the last chapter I try to take a look forward into the future of ritual.

My methodology is – just as for anyone who writes about their professional specialty – determined in large part by my profession as a priest of the Christian Community. Because of the freedom afforded by this position and great tolerance regarding other forms of belief, I went far beyond the boundaries of the Christian Community, anthroposophy (which is often wrongly identified with the Christian Community) and Christian theology, in an effort to attain insight and an overview of the diversity of ritual forms.

What is ritual?

Before we begin our exploration into the origin of various forms of ritual, I want to focus on the concept of ritual. Wherever you look in the history of humanity, every culture, every time period, every country has had its own forms of ritual. Our words 'culture' and 'cult' (original meaning: divine service, worship) come from the Latin verb *colere,* which means cultivating the earth. In the first few chapters we will see that the original forms of ritual had everything to do with cultivating the earth.

No culture ever developed without ritual. In many cultures we can follow this development exactly. In the ancient theocracies, life in society was organised and guided from temples and mystery places. The altar was experienced as the place from which human beings derived their right to exist. 'Stronger than an impregnable fortress is the altar,' says an old Greek proverb. And in the Jewish tradition the worst idea of destruction was that the Holy of Holies would be abandoned and fall into illegitimate hands, surrendered to heathens on the day that the daily offerings would be suspended (Dan.12:11).

The altar is the place where the unborn and the dead, the visible and invisible world, saints and hierarchies, God and human beings come together. At all times and in all cultures, however, the origin of the ritual service at the altar was not viewed as arising on earth, but in heaven.

Ritual has its roots in the priesthood of the angels, for in the spiritual world stands the invisible altar where day and night the hierarchies bring offerings and worship God. The earthly priesthood is no more (but also no less) than a shadow of this. The spiritual world can inspire earthly ritual and, through the priest, help carry and order life on earth. The task of the priest is to build a bridge between heaven and earth: hence the title *pontifex,* which means bridge builder. Old forms of organisation in society were therefore generally viewed as reflections of the order of the hierarchies in heaven. (The word 'hierarchy', derived from Greek, means holy order.) In its original, pure form, the ordering of society always took place in accordance with the fundamental esoteric law of analogy: As above, so below.[1] The fact that this law was corrupted in the course of history and is no longer of our time, needs no further amplification.

In the course of this exposition on ritual it will become clear how in our time ritual content and individual freedom can go together. But separated from spiritual reality, without the help of heavenly liturgy, earthly ritual remains a human piece of work. In Chapter 13, 'Hierarchies and Adversary Powers', I have written more extensively on heavenly liturgy.

Initially a scheme might be helpful in forming an overview of all the elements that are part of the celebration of a ritual. The very distinction between heavenly and earthly ritual demonstrates that there is an immense distance between two worlds that has to be bridged. Of old this reality was viewed as a heavenly ladder. In a dream Jacob, one of the patriarchs of the Jewish people, saw a ladder whose top reached into heaven. At the top stood God; along the ladder angels went up and down between heaven and earth.

The human being, Jacob, was lying asleep at the foot of the angel ladder. For ritual we can complete this picture with the following:

God
Angelic hierarchies and the angel of the congregation
Saints, those who have died and those not yet born
Priest
Congregation
Temple or church
Ritual substances
Creation

In ancient times it was known that between the world of God and the earthly world there is an abyss.* Those who were initiated in the old mysteries had to bridge this dizzying chasm. In addition to the way of initiation, which was accessible only to a few, there was another way between heaven and earth. Medieval tradition speaks of a term from alchemy, the *aurea catena*, the golden chain that connects heaven and earth. On its way from heaven to earth the overwhelming light of the Godhead is tempered. Humanity cannot bear the unbroken light of the Godhead, 'He who sees God dies.' In 'sacred sheaths'[2] this light is veiled and made accessible. The sheaths not only serve the human being who reconnects *(re-ligion* means reconnection) with the divine world, but they also serve the creation which has been estranged from its divine origin. For this reason, in countless forms of ritual, substances were used that were consecrated or transubstantiated. In this way, the earth and the creation also participate in this reconnection. Ritual may thus become a factor of culture.

That this is not just something of the past but is current even now, is illustrated by a conversation Martha Heimeran (1895–1965), one of the founders of the Christian Community, had with Rudolf Steiner (1861–1925). Heimeran said to Steiner, 'I want to commit myself to the renewal of culture.' Steiner's answer was, 'If you want to renew culture, you have to begin with the ritual.' I think we should not imagine this renewal of culture right away on a large scale but, to begin with, in individual human beings.

* For instance, in the old Norwegian tale, *The Dream Song of Olaf Åsteson,* which dates back to about 400 AD, the Gjallard Bridge over the abyss is described.

For instance, someone who had lived for years with the Act of Consecration of Man – the central sacrament in the Christian Community – said, 'Because of the Act of Consecration of Man I have learned to lead a listening life.' Listening to the ritual brought about in this person an ability to develop a different culture of listening in daily life. A capacity had grown in him to hear what lives behind the words, to glean from the course of events how he could stand in a healthy relationship to those events.

Also, the acts performed in true ritual correspond directly with the heavenly liturgy. Worship, reverence and prayer form part of the language with which the hierarchies speak to the Godhead. Some of the words have even been taken directly from heavenly ritual. The 'Sanctus' in the Latin mass is derived from the heavenly vision of the prophet Isaiah, who witnessed the Seraphim worshipping God and exclaiming, 'Holy, holy, holy is the LORD of hosts; the whole earth is full of his glory' (Isa.6:3).[3] In this connection Dionysius the Areopagite spoke of 'the theology of the Seraphim.'

After this brief introduction we are going to search for the oldest known traditions of earthly ritual. In this process we will also follow the traces of ancient forms of ritual, for which archeologists can provide some clues.

1

Forms of Worship in the Stone Age

From the moment the gates of Paradise were closed, the Old Testament speaks of ritual. Beginning in the fourth chapter of Genesis offerings are mentioned: Cain offered the fruits of the earth to Yahweh, and Abel made an animal offering with the sacrificial smoke that rises. These are indications that ritual has existed since the most ancient past. In addition to this example from the Old Testament – which we will return to more extensively – rituals and offerings are mentioned in many creation stories and myths. These stories date back to prehistoric times of which no outer visible traces can be found.

In the twentieth century, anthropology went so far as to assert (in a movement that was called the school of myths and rites) that all myths have a cultic origin. In this theory the baby was thrown out with the bathwater, because this anthropological school had the following view: the stories about gods have sprung from the imagination of the priests and shamans who performed the rituals. By their ritual acts they arrived at fantastic imaginations about gods.

At any rate, wherever you look, ritual is as old as humanity. Actually, we need to go back even farther. Ritual has its origin not in the world of human beings, but in the world of the gods: a world in which gods make offerings to gods in the archetype of ritual.

North and south

The first examples of ritual can be found in megalithic cultures* that have left their traces everywhere. We can make a distinction between the megalithic culture in northern countries and the forms of building and ritual that developed in southern countries. In Egypt,

* Greek *megas* means large, *lithos* stone.

for example, we find imposing temples that led people inward. In most cases the central part is enclosed and dark. In Europe, especially Ireland, England and Brittany (France), we see megalithic structures that are open on all sides, and have no, or hardly any closed spaces, while the Egyptian temple, literally and figuratively, led one inward. The megalithic cultures in Europe have a connection with the cosmos. In recent decades, research in this realm has generated interesting new material, as will be shown later in this chapter.

Differences in culture and ritual between what happened in a country like Egypt (southern culture) and in western Europe (northern culture) were noticed already by the Greek historian Herodotus (484–424 BC). In his *Histories* he wrote, 'As the sky in Egypt is different from elsewhere, as the stream is different there from other streams, so are also the manners and customs of the Egyptians almost in all respects opposite to those of other cultures.'

At the sources of these cultures we find two different forms of ancient mysteries, the southern and the northern mysteries.[1] The southern mysteries (those in Egypt, for instance) led inward; the northern ones led into nature and the cosmos. We find traces of stone monuments (northern mysteries) first in Ireland, England and Brittany but they were spread all over Europe, far into eastern Europe, the Crimea and the Caucasus. In the south they spread to Sardinia and North Africa, even into Palestine. After Carbon-14 (a radioactive isotope of carbon) dating had been perfected, these stone monuments were found to have been erected from about 3000 BC, the era in which the great structures in Egypt arose. However, for a long time they were the step-children of archeology. What was built in the north was much less spectacular than what the southern mysteries produced, like such wonders as the ziggurats of Mesopotamia and the pyramids, sphinxes and rock tombs of Egypt.

A big difference with the southern cultures is that writing had already been developed before 3000 BC, and everything was documented from A to Z; as on the walls of temples and pyramids, the Egyptian Book of the Dead, etc. In Europe writing developed much later, which is the reason why it was thought that there was hardly any culture there. The stone monuments in Europe generated little interest among archeologists until late in the twentieth century. Actually, for centuries the investigators of the megalithic cultures did little more than measure inch by inch the sizes of all those stones. But this didn't help them at all in gaining insight into the significance of this culture.

An expression of the helpless attitude regarding the megalithic cultures is the conclusion Daniel Defoe reached in 1705: 'All that can be said of them is that here they are!' In 1800, the poet Lord Byron became rather frustrated by the monument of Stonehenge and exclaimed, 'But what the devil is it?' In 1872 all that Samuel Ferguson, an Irish antiquarian, could come up with was the statement, 'Rough stone monuments.' In brief, people were always stopped by the outside and were unable to penetrate to the significance of megalithic culture. All people could see in those places was piles of stones, whereas their real meaning can only be discovered out of the nature of which they are a part.

Only in the 1980s did archeologists arrive at the insight that there is indeed something like 'megalithic astronomy', and that these megaliths have a relationship with the cosmos. When these stones began to be viewed in relation to the landscape, rivers, hills, to sunrise and sunset, the insight grew that such places had been observatories of the positions of, for instance, the sun and moon.

In Aberdeenshire, Scotland, there is a badly damaged stone circle named Balquhain, of which tradition tells that the new moon was welcomed there with prayer. This tradition had always been brushed aside by researchers, but later it was discovered that there is indeed a connection with the cosmos and positions of the moon.

The sanctuary was ingeniously composed of twelve standing stones that all had a specific colour and form. In between, a recumbent stone was placed, a gigantic monolith that – as it was possible to reconstruct – was perfectly levelled by means of little wedges put underneath it. People created an artificial horizon in antiquity, for the recumbent stone repeats the line of the horizon behind it; even the forms of a hill had been formed in it with a little rise and indentation, so that the stone was in perfect harmony with the landscape around it.

Geological research showed that this recumbent stone had been brought from many miles away. How that was done remains a mystery. When the other stones were investigated it turned out that one was of red granite, a second of black basalt, a third of white granite, a fourth of red quartzite, in brief, exquisite stones found far away, that in their original configuration must have been a surprisingly colourful sight.

On these stones, which were very consciously placed in a sequence from high to low, engraved rock art was found, but only on those stones on which moon positions could be read.

From the 1980s archeologists began to look for alignments, horizon lines, and it was discovered that if instead of facing the menhirs, you turn your back to them and look at the landscape, the stones begin to 'speak'. Following this discovery, the stones are said to have a front and a back: they have an orientation. It is possible to recognise and identify many positions of the sunrise in all those different stone monuments, such as the summer and winter solstice on 21 June and 21 December, and the spring and autumnal equinoxes. But there are also other indications, like sunrise or sunset on certain festival days that we no longer celebrate, like the spring festival of Beltane on 1 May, or the harvest festival Lughnasadh on 1 August.

Five thousand years ago Samhain, All Souls, was celebrated on November 1. Almost no one today knows that we owe All Souls Day not to Christian tradition, but to the most ancient forms of ritual in the Stone Age. In brief, the timing of all those characteristic Celtic festivals can now be reconstructed and recognised in various stone monuments. This is true not only for positions of the sun, but also of the moon. It was this discovery that caused a breakthrough in the research into stone circles.

The first conclusion was that these sacred places were connected with the cosmos, and that three thousand years before Christ humanity in these regions day and night lived with the cosmos. The other discovery, which had been made much earlier, was that in these holy places there were often human remains, but not in all of them. It is a misconception that all stone monuments were cemeteries. Apparently there was a connection between stone circles, the cosmos and the dead. The three have something in common. This could be recognised because many bodies that were later buried in a cairn (a conical pile of stones of a pre-Celtic tomb), had the feet pointing to the rising sun. Even the dead were 'oriented'.

Thousands of miles to the west, the Dakota Indians in North America had the custom of placing the dead on a rise with their feet to the rising sun. There is a connection between what those different peoples knew or thought about dead souls and the cosmos. Even today the Navajo Indians say, 'The dead travel along the course of the sun.'

As above, so below

The fundamental esoteric law, 'as above, so below', which was referred to in the Introduction, was in a certain sense confirmed by a discovery first published in 2007.[2] The archeologist Allard Mees was exploring a long-known early Celtic funeral mound, Magdalenenberg, in southern Germany. The principal tomb was dated by dendrochronology to the year 616 BC. Magdalenenberg is the largest funeral mound in western Europe known to date. In the centre of the mound the tomb with the remains of a ruler was found, which also contained a chariot. Around it the hill has 136 additional graves.

Mees, who had studied astronomy, by chance noticed the remarkable arrangement of the other tombs in the mound. In the pattern of the graves he recognised the forms of astronomical constellations as they were thousands of years ago. Superimposing the constellations as they appeared in 616 BC on a plan of the graves, there is an astonishing correspondence between the pattern of the graves and that of the constellations. More than thirteen constellations can be recognised in the pattern of the graves, without any effort (see Figure 1, over page).

The starry sky that is shown here in the pattern of the graves corresponds with all the constellations that were visible above the horizon at the time of the summer solstice, which then took place between 26 and 29 June. Even the brightness of the constellations was reflected in the graves. For instance, the brightest summer star Vega in the constellation of Lyra is pictured in the most important double grave in the Magdalenenberg.

In this double grave a woman was buried with a metal girdle showing sun and star motifs, presumably the grave of the young wife of the ruler. We witness, as it were, the creation of the starry sky in the pattern of the graves – as above, so below.

We find this principle both in culture and in forms of ritual. Especially in funerals in antiquity, culture and ritual were still fully linked.

On the Magdalenenberg funeral mound the relationship to the features of the night sky were also pictured in another aspect by rows of poles. These poles were situated in the mound and formed part of the whole picture of the arrangement from the beginning. Mees discovered that these rows of wooden poles were oriented on

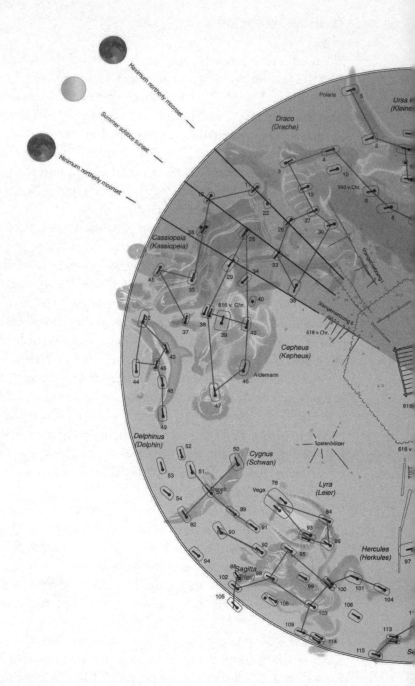

Figure 1. Constellations and the graves of Magdalenenberg, southern Germany.

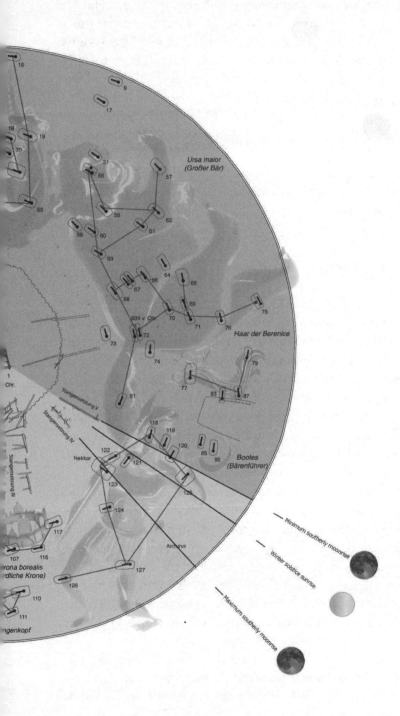

the most important positions of the moon. Calculating the movements of the moon at that time (around 616 BC) he found that these posts located the turning points of the extreme rising and setting positions of the moon which are related to the moon nodes. These turning points recur in a rhythm of 18.61 years, so that after this period the position of moonrise and moonset are located in the same place again. Orientation on moon nodes is only found from the Hallstatt period onwards (c. 800–400 BC). It is a new development that cannot be found in earlier cultures.

The whole construction and arrangement of the funeral mound at Magdalenenberg has a double orientation: on the turning points of both the moon and the sun.

Legends and traditions

Despite human remains sometimes being found, it is a mistake to think that stone circles were also cemeteries. In many places, in the midst of the stone circles small open areas were discovered, into which fertile soil was brought – in one place on the Orkney Islands even seeds of fruit. These are places that were excavated and then filled again with different kinds of remarkably fertile soil. Apparently stone monuments had to do not only with death, but also with fertility and with life. Another aspect that points in that direction is that countless stone circles and dolmen are located close to water.

We find a peculiar motif that may perhaps help us understand the ways in which people regarded stones in those times, and how they related them to the cosmos. Legends tell in various ways that the stones that were placed there were alive, and even – this legend occurs in many places – that they once a year secretly walk away from their places and submerge themselves in water. 'Living' stones! The presumption is that there was a ritual with water during which the stones were submerged, but in the same places there are also traces of gigantic fires. A water ritual *and* a fire ritual.

After a long search I finally found a reprint of a little book, *The Secret Commonwealth of Elves, Fauns and Fairies,* written in 1691 by a church minister, Robert Kirk. This man, who lived in Scotland, described that the stone monuments were viewed in his time as fairy rings, places where nature beings dwelled. Marina Warner, who wrote the introduction to the reprint, made a curious leap from this old idea to her own time. She wrote, 'In 2005 *The Times* published a report that a real estate broker in Scotland was prevented from subdividing land he had bought in order to build a few houses on it, because a fairy stone, a monolith, was standing there. The article had the title "Fairies stop developer's bulldozers".' The author made a joke about it and wrote that the belief of the local population is something like Mac feng shui. Feng shui is the Chinese art of sensing something spiritual in the environment.

The stones that were erected there are, according to popular tradition, living beings, dwelling places for the invisible world, humans or giants. One of the oldest names of Stonehenge is *choreia gigantum,* dance of the giants. Other names also point to a kind of dance that was performed there. Stones that dance or make music. They received illustrious names like Nine Maidens, Twelve Apostles, Piper Stones. They were stones that were dwelling places of invisible beings, and – I am making a big leap to the Holy Land – even became the home of a divinity, a *Beth-El.* For Jacob in fact did something similar to what the druids did. On his flight from Esau he took a stone, erected it and poured oil over the head of the stone making it Beth-El, a house of God (Gen.28:18f). Stones as the house of God, temple or offering place on earth – that is the oldest recognisable form of ritual.

It is truly fascinating to try to live into these views of the world of stones and become sensitive to the stones. What do the stones speak? What do they hear? An old proverb says, 'Do not lie; the earth hears it.' The earth has a sense organ for what human beings do to her.

One day during an Act of Consecration I was fascinated by the floor, which was inlaid with pebbles, and I received an inspiration for a poem. It was in the 1980s when I had just begun my work as a priest when, seated in a church by the side of the altar, I had a strong impression of the floor of the space. Sometimes it is as if the area around you comes to life in a certain way, as if it takes something in, becomes aware of what human beings do, think and speak there.

The stones have seen it
The stones become eyes
When I walk on the earth
When I walk with Christ
The stones have seen it,
The stones shall preserve it.

What came into being there in poetic form can be related by clairvoyant people in much finer nuances. Annie Gerding, who became known in the Netherlands for her clairvoyant observations of nature, told me once of her experiences with the stone monuments in the Dutch province of Drenthe. Around these stones live spiritual beings, nature beings who remember what took place there centuries ago, not in a sense of any outer registration, but an uninterrupted consciousness of what took place there.

The druid culture

There are great differences between the forms of the structures built by the northern and southern mystery streams. In the Stone Age small communities lived in Europe that led an isolated existence. In contrast with 'massive' cultures such as in Egypt, Persia and Babylonia, where one leader, Pharaoh or priest-king directed everything in a pyramidal system, in Europe there were only fragmented, separate states and kingdoms with an overwhelming variety of cultures and forms of stone monuments. In every region, the stone monuments are oriented slightly differently. There were separate tribes and languages, local architectural traditions, but in all those cultures and rituals there was one common denominator. Most of the stone monuments were the work of the druids. They were the ones who determined everything through their social position: agriculture, cattle raising, justice, ritual, home building, stone circles, veneration of the dead. Everything came together through the druids, the spiritual leaders of the culture.

Julius Caesar (100–44 BC) related that a person had to be educated and trained for twenty years to become a druid, because his position was so all-encompassing. They inspired the entire culture. They needed an astronomical calendar for this, for there was no calendar that showed when the sun would stand at its highest position, or when the cattle had to be brought in again, or when it was time to sow. This was determined by means of the stone monuments, megalithic astronomy, that indicated when the sun had reached its highest point, and what the consequences were for the earth, for the cultures, for agriculture, for cattle etc. The druid culture was the unity in multiplicity, which in a hidden way penetrated and inspired everything.

We find the most complete description of the druid culture in Rudolf Steiner's work; he became acquainted with this culture unexpectedly in the summer of 1923. He was invited to lecture during a summer conference at Ilkley, Yorkshire, England and at Penmaenmawr in Wales. At that time relatively little was known about stone monuments. Steiner must have arrived without advance knowledge from literature. In Ilkley he was deeply impressed when he walked up on the moors and found old stone monuments. He could 'read' them with his trained clairvoyant gaze. He recognised what was hidden behind the outer appearance and said that what took place in druid culture had engraved itself into the spiritual atmosphere of that spot. Imaginations, images of druid ritual had remained behind and made permanent connections with the atmosphere.

Shortly after his return to Switzerland, when he expressed time and again how deeply impressed he was by these stone monuments, Rudolf Steiner made a pastel drawing (Figure 2, over page). There is a recognisable similarity to the photograph of the stones at Ilkley. The photograph shows lowlands with a hill; then the landscape rises to a plateau with the Swastika Stone (not visible in this picture), followed by a second plateau. The three stone altars in the pastel drawing stand in those places at Ilkley.

Steiner depicted more than the outer landscape, using different colours to show something essential. But first of all the composition is important: the lowlands, the first plateau, the second plateau, and the sky above them. In the drawing we can recognise three human figures. Below, in blue, someone is squatting, apparently surrounded by gigantic blue crystals. By the altar on the first plateau a priest in a light red vestment stands, bowing towards the altar and the plain below. Finally, higher up where the three altars are standing, a priest figure in a light red vestment, is shown in 'higher spheres'.

Figure 2. Druid Stones, *pastel drawing by Rudolf Steiner.*

Steiner depicts more than outer reality. Above the two red priestly figures we can see a luminous cloud, an aura. Perhaps the most surprising thing in the whole drawing is a cross in the form of a spiral on the lower altar. For clairvoyant consciousness this is the imagination of a chakra or lotus flower.

In ancient India seven clairvoyant sense-organs called lotus flowers or chakras were recognised. There may be an eighth that is located above the human figure, but that one falls out of the spiritual tradition described by Steiner. One of the chakras, the four-petaled lotus

Figure 3. Stone sanctuary near Ilkley, England.

flower, is also known as the swastika. It has to do with fertilisation and procreation. The Nazis appropriated this symbol and literally turned it around by pointing the four arms in the opposite directions. We find the swastika in many cultures as a symbol of initiation. Steiner used the symbol in his mystery drama, *The Guardian of the Threshold.* The symbol of the four-petaled lotus flower forms the centre of the seal Steiner designed for this mystery drama.

In the pastel drawing we see three different persons in three different worlds. On the lower right is a figure squatting in a world of crystal; in the middle is the priest who is bending before the altar with the lotus flower. We find the swastika form engraved in the rocks at Ilkley, the Swastika Stone. Steiner showed the spiritual archetype of it and said:

What do you see in this sign when you stand in front of such a stone? You see the words that lived in the heart of the druid priest: See, the eye of the senses beholds the mountains, the places of human beings; the eye of the spirit, the revolving lotus flower (for that is what the swastika signifies), beholds the hearts of human beings, beholds the inner world of the soul. Through this beholding, said the druid priest, I want to be connected with those who have been entrusted to me in community.[3]

It was the purpose of druid training to become clairvoyant by living intensely with nature, to bring these spiritual sense organs latent in every human being, into movement, to make them perceptive and with their aid to know the mysteries of the depths, the mysteries of the heights, and the mysteries of the middle. It is not arbitrary that three places are pictured here. The druid priest in the depths connected himself with the earth, penetrating through the world of crystals into the inmost essence of the earth, where spiritual powers and cosmic will are working. The druid priest standing by the three high altars connected himself with the mysteries of the heights, with the mysteries of cosmic intelligence. (But we have to understand the word 'intelligence' in its original meaning. In the Middle Ages, the world of the archangels was meant: in the School of Chartres the word was used to indicate the archangels.) Finally, the middle druid was connected to the mystery of the human being who, between heaven and earth, between the heights and the depths, took his own place in the world.

A month later, Rudolf Steiner spoke about the heights, the depths and the middle.[4] Word for word this lecture parallels the description of the druid mysteries. Everything Steiner had seen and recognised in the druid mysteries now led in this lecture to an appeal to learn to know the spirit in nature. The goal of the druid priests was not to know the spiritual world on the inward path, but to know the spirit in nature outside. And this, said Steiner, is also in our time a legitimate way into the spiritual world. We should not live in seclusion from the rest of humanity, but learn with open ears and open eyes to know the workings of the spiritual world in nature, the workings of the Lord of the Elements.

Friedrich Rittelmeyer once asked Steiner, 'If we imagine that for one person Christ is far away, and for another very near, how in this time can I find true access to Christ?' Steiner answered, 'That is only possible if one learns to experience Christ in the course of the year.' Living into the course of the seasons is the surest way to Christ. With this a task was given to the Christian Community to cultivate a connection between Christianity and nature. Or, as Steiner sometimes formulated it for the founders of the Christian Community, 'You have the task of Christianising natural science.'

Shortly after his visit to Ilkley and Penmaenmawr, Steiner gave a lecture to the construction workers at the Goetheanum in Dornach. In response to a question from one of the workers he sketched a picture of the development of forms of ritual from the most distant past until now. Because this approach contains important points for the content of this book, I want to consider it in some detail here. Steiner started with the experience he had with the stone circles in England shortly before, and concluded after creating a picture of the druid rituals, 'So you have a rite here which essentially consisted in people wanting to bring the spiritual element from the cosmos down to the earth for their social and life situations.'[5] This form, which originated in the ancient theocracy, can no longer be practised in our time. At the same time however, Steiner showed with the aid of several examples that elements from these original forms of ritual have found their way to later forms, even into our time. The mere fact, for instance, that the altar is oriented in the direction of the rising sun shows a connection with the cosmos. Sun and moon play an important role in the symbolism of the Christian ritual in the Most Blessed Sacrament, when the consecrated host is shown (see Chapter 5, 'Mithraism').

For our time it is not sufficient that a ritual corresponds with cosmic laws. Most of all this is due to the fact that humanity has emancipated itself from its cosmic origin – with all the complications this has caused. There is no way back. All efforts toward restoration of the old order lead to the necessity for humanity to hand over its laboriously acquired freedom again. In a certain sense in pre-Christian cultures the human being was a marionette. We were led by kings and priests who, in their turn, were led by the laws of the cosmos and spiritual world. The ancient cultures of, for example, Egypt, Israel or

India were organised like gigantic ant heaps or colonies of bees. Each human being had a pre-ordained role from which they could not be freed.

With the coming of Christ on earth individual freedom began to play a role, also in religious life. Not once did Christ use the word obedience, in sharp contrast with the message of the Old Testament. As the language of the Old Testament speaks of commands and obedience, so Christ speaks of the word and of hearing. In the parable of the sower this connection is recognisable from beginning to end. Human freedom to choose to take in the word or not plays a crucial role: is it ignored or does it fall onto good earth? Christ leaves human beings free like no other. The ultimate consequence of this is his suffering and death on the cross. When it became a state religion to a great extent this freedom was nullified, thus robbing Christianity of an essential characteristic.

When Rudolf Steiner spoke in the twentieth century of new, future forms of ritual and religion, he followed this fundamental characteristic. In the lecture to the construction workers mentioned above, he said:

Today this way of developing a ritual out of the inmost life
of the human being can at most only be a beginning. It was
through the druid rites that people knew how to garland the
bull, set the time for the bull festival, walk the bull through the
local village so that reproduction would be properly regulated,
and if we develop a rite that will serve to develop perception
in the spirit sustained by the cerebellum, we shall know what
needs to be done in social life ... When it can be admitted that
we must first of all know in the spirit what has to happen in the
human world, because it flows from the universe, we will at last
have a proper social science, and this will be something willed
from the cosmic world that surrounds us.[6]

With these words we have come full circle.

Old and new forms of ritual are characterised both by their own nature and by their (partial) mutual relationship. In the end, both are in harmony with the cosmos. But in our time ritual will have to speak first of all to the inner world of human beings, to the 'hidden holy of holies' of their I. Out of the I that forges a connection with Christ out of its own free will, we can make a beginning with what Steiner called the 'royal art of the future.' In other words, forms for social life in which spiritual freedom is guaranteed for every individual human being.

In the following chapters we will follow the religious and ritual developments of several cultures. As has already become clear from the foregoing we rarely witness a complete break with the old, but a development that goes step by step, although sometimes in great leaps. We mostly see organic development that goes through metamorphoses.

2

Nature Religion and Ancestor Worship

With the description of megalithic cultures we have by no means exhausted the forms of pre-Christian cultures. In this chapter I will try to show something of the origin and development of pagan forms of culture. After all, even in our time there are many peoples and tribes that practise this form of religion.

The earliest stage of religion is usually called animism: all existence is ensouled and permeated by life. Every child goes through this stage anew, even if they live in a world that has no use for their ways of viewing things and acting with them. As down-to-earth, critical adults we often look at their little world with pity or amusement, but our belief in it is questionable. When my youngest grandchild has to put away his toys in the evening, every block gets a kiss before it is put in the box. Little children are animists; not only plants and animals but also dolls, tables and chairs – even the whole world – are filled with life.

Only in exceptional situations does this way of seeing the world remain in adults. A handicapped man once vented his rage by hitting the cover of a grand piano with his fist, which resulted in an impressive sound effect. After his fury had spent itself he lifted the cloth covering the piano and caressed the wood, to make it good again. Primitive? If we observe our own feelings in similar situations we may well recognise such tendencies. At one time we all lived in a fairy-tale world where everything came to life.

For the young child the step from the visible to the invisible world is effortless. This is mostly because the child is still connected with its spiritual origin – just as this was self-evident for everyone in antiquity. 'Where there are children, there is a golden age,' Novalis wrote in his *Fragments*. For the clairvoyant gaze the outer world is nothing but a veil, an externally visible texture that hides the essential being. The experience of atavistic clairvoyance is basically the same as the countless forms of natural clairvoyance that occur in children in our time.

In the Egyptian-Chaldean cultural epoch – Rudolf Steiner also called it the third post-Atlantean epoch – the original nature religion spread far and wide. Although the Jewish people in the time of the Old Testament increasingly explored their own inner world, we also find – even in the Old Testament – strong expressions of an animistic world image: nature is everywhere permeated with the divine. Everything is ensouled. A picture of this form of perception was given by Rudolf Steiner when he described what Chaldeans or Egyptians saw in certain natural phenomena. When they looked at foxglove they began to blush; and looking at the poisonous herb henbane they went pale. Visible nature evoked strong reactions right into their physiology. The sight of a twisting snake caused violent inner agitation.

Because nature and the human soul were 'communicating vessels', the observation of an animal evoked animal-like forces in the human being. For the consciousness of those times it was generally understood that the snake was the craftiest of all animals (see Gen.3:1). In our time a clairvoyant can still recognise which animal forces are working in the soul. For instance, someone who had let himself be guided by faultless intuitions in his associations with people once said, 'If someone is not reliable I see the figure of a fox in him. In some men a bull appears. If someone is a very clear thinker I see the figure of a horse around him.' Without being aware of it we often drag a whole zoo behind us!

Nature religion in the psalms

I would like to illustrate this early stage of religion with a few examples from the psalms. When we explore the psalms with their many images of nature word by word, we discover that the psalmist was generally able to recognise the spiritual essence behind phenomena. In Psalm 104 all of nature has become an expression of the Godhead:[1]

> Bless the LORD, O my soul!
> O LORD, my God, thou art very great!
> Thou art clothed with honor and majesty,

God exceeds all limits of human comprehension. He is 'very great', he permeates the entire creation, he is clothed in 'a radiance that truly shines out from him' as we could render the Hebrew expression *hod we-hadar*. The word *hod* is translated into Latin as *confessio:* his inner being shines out as a 'confession'. The word *hadar* indicates the divine radiance. But both words point to a supersensible reality – not yet a visible reality. In the next verses of this psalm the Godhead gradually comes to manifestation in visible nature:

> Who coverest thyself with light as with a garment,
> Who has stretched out the heavens like a tent,
> Who hast laid the beams of thy chambers on the waters.

The psalmist uses imagery here that leads from inner to outer: garment – tent – chambers. But up to this point we still see the spiritual reality *behind* the physical: the 'waters' are here the 'waters above the firmament' of which Genesis 1:7 speaks. It is the world of the streaming life forces that is meant here. Only then does the psalmist describe the way that the Godhead goes to visible nature:

> Who makest the clouds thy chariot,
> Who ridest on the wings of the wind,
> Who makest the winds thy messengers [Greek *angeloi*],
> Fire and flame thy ministers.

All the elements appear as 'vehicles' of the Godhead. For the religious constitution of the time the clouds were infinitely more than signs of the weather; they were messengers of the workings of God. The winds were ruled by winged beings, angels. The blazing fire was God's minister or servant. The highest hierarchy was viewed as consisting in fiery beings; the word seraphim means the flaming ones, the purifying ones.

In the first sentence of the psalm God appears in all his greatness, as Being. In the description of spiritual light, heaven and 'waters' he reveals himself. Next his workings come to expression in the elements of clouds, wind and fire. Only then does the psalm arrive at the tangible world:

> Thou didst set the earth on its foundations,
> So that it should never be shaken.

The earth is the condensed, definitive work. In these four concepts of being, revelation, workings, and creation, the long road of the Creator becomes visible. Rudolf Steiner described the stages of the creation in these four concepts.[2] It is not difficult to recognise these stages in the psalm, although they are represented not in concepts but in pictures.

That the earth is the 'final product' of the Creator is told more explicitly in Psalm 95:5:

> For his hands formed the dry land.

The Greek text has the word *eplasan* here: plasticised, kneaded. After this process from heaven to earth, which resembles a repetition of Genesis, Psalm 104 describes in all detail the visible creation, permeated by the breath of God. The message is: nothing in creation was left to chance.

In the next, the fourth post-Atlantean cultural epoch, the Greco-Roman period, in which intellectual thinking is reduced to concepts, humanity lost this natural connection with nature. The Greek writer Plutarch (c. AD 46–120) related that in his time a ship sailed along the coast in the Mediterranean from which it was continually proclaimed, 'The great god Pan is dead!' Pan was the god in the shape of a goat who revealed himself in thunderstorms, in the oppressive heat of the afternoon, in sudden natural phenomena. His sudden appearances caused 'pan-ic' among people.

The Greek word *pan* means 'everything', a concept that was seen as connected with the god Pan. He went accompanied by an army of nymphs and satyrs (kind of demons of the forest). But the Godhead who used to reveal himself in nature has disappeared from it. Human beings are thrown back onto themselves and nature is silent. In northern Europe the same was indicated by the death of Baldur, the god of nature.

Christ and nature

With the coming of the Messiah on earth – particularly with his descent into hell and his resurrection – something comes to life in nature which had been close to dying. The dying earth existence is brought to new life by the Risen One. Without this re-enlivening the creation would have perished. This was expressed in drastic terms in a medieval Easter hymn:

> Had He not been raised,
> The whole world would have perished.

This renewal, which did not happen once for all time but takes place every year anew, is very subtly and playfully expressed by the Swedish author Selma Lagerlöf. One of her stories tells of the abbot of a monastery, Father Anselm, who begins the midnight mass in the walled garden of the monastery, 'He wanted that nature would participate in the great joy brought to all creatures at Christmas Eve.'[3] With all the monks he goes through the garden in ceremonial vestments, incense in one hand, holy water in the other, while he sings the hymns of the birth of God's Son. He censes the garden and sprinkles holy water on the dead, frozen ground. At that moment something changes in the air. A south wind starts up and in a few gusts wipes away the cold and the snow. From under the snow green grass appears. Buds that were tightly closed in the ice, unfold and open. A sweet air of spring fills the garden. Allured by the spring air, birds come from miles away and sing to the birth of the Creator. A squirrel comes in over the wall and frolics from branch to branch in the trees. Abbot Anselm opens the gate and from all directions animals from the forest stream in and become guests in this midnight mass in the midst of nature. The most miraculous of all, tells the legend, is the arrival of the stork of the monastery, who was thought to be far away in Egypt, where he goes every winter. Suddenly there is the swishing of wings – the stork flies in carrying in its beak a little bottle with the elixir of life, nature's Christmas gift to Abbot Anselm. That is a colourful, imaginative expression for 'the re-enlivening of the dying earth existence', as it is expressed in the Creed of the Christian Community.

Also in the well-known legend from the same book about the Christmas Rose, nature is in a certain sense the principal character. In a remote forest, where only robbers live, nature blooms on Christmas Eve and, as a sign of the renewal of life, leaves the snow-white Christmas Rose behind. Those who regard such stories as fables and pious stories, have not really understood them. Of course Selma Lagerlöf, who had the gift of second sight, was not talking about outer miracles. If at Christmas Eve people are able to behold the spiritual reality behind nature, they would see how the earth is suffused in light.

One of my friends, whose custom was to read this story by Selma Lagerlöf to his family every year at Christmas, told me that nature beings came from far and near and filled the whole room when he read this story to his family for the first time. And even though after this overwhelming experience he could no longer see them appear with his own eyes, he still experienced every year anew the magic of the story. In such experiences, which are by no means unique today, something can be recognised of the reality of the oldest, and perhaps also the newest, forms of religion: nature is permeated with spiritual forces that ask us for recognition and acknowledgement. But this form of 'animism' only becomes real when not the creation, but the Creator himself is worshipped. Selma Lagerlöf is not speaking of a return to some primitive nature religion, but of the recognition of Christ who is coming again and who suffuses nature with his radiance as 'the Lord of the heavenly forces upon earth', (as it is expressed in the Creed of the Christian Community).

Ancestor worship

Ancestor worship, the oldest form of religion, can be approached in a similar manner. On the one hand, this is an area that might be viewed as a closed chapter, but on the other hand, the right kind of relationship with the dead also harbours the seed of new developments in religious and ritual life.

Rudolf Steiner remarked concerning this form of religion, 'Ancestor worship, veneration of the ancestors, was indeed the first religion. The memory had in a sensed stayed alive.'[4] From our own experience we know that memories may be very differently coloured, or may have faded. Some memories can come close to reality or even evoke it; others lead a semi-conscious, unconscious or subconscious existence. But if we call up in our memory someone who was dear to us, we may sometimes have an experience of their presence – as if the real memory makes an appeal on the dead person. Memory is a capacity that can reproduce, that is literally, produce anew. We know that in ancient times people's memory was much more strongly developed than it is now. How else could they have handed down fairy tales, myths and legends orally for centuries?

When the Finnish philologist Elias Lönnrot discovered the Kalevala epic in the nineteenth century, he found people who could effortlessly remember hundreds of verses. Similarly in ancestor worship people in their memory climbed the ladder to those who had died, beginning with the recently deceased who were immediately remembered and in a way still tangibly present, to the world of their ancestors, and back to the patriarchs of the people. Much more literally than we usually understand the Old Testament, the people of Israel were able to say, 'We have Abraham as our father.'

The times of going to sleep and waking up are traditionally the best moments to enter the world of the dead. That is also the world of the etheric or life forces, which is the 'ground' of those who have died. One of the meditations for the dead in a verse by Rudolf Steiner begins with the words:

> Angels, Archangels and Archai
> In the Ether weaving,
> Receive man's web of Destiny.[5]

Through ancestor worship, through the world of the dead, people also came in touch with the world of the hierarchies. In this way those who have died build a bridge between the human world and that of the hierarchies. We will come back to this principle more extensively in Chapter 5, 'Mithraism' and in Chapter 12, 'The Unborn and the Dead in Ritual'.

There are still some highly cultivated forms of ancestor worship in cultures today. An important record of this is in John G. Neihardt's book, *Black Elk Speaks*, which first appeared in 1932. For many days

Neihardt, an ethnologist, had conversations with the chief of the Sioux Indians, Black Elk, in which the latter described his 'visions of the other world' that appeared to him with the aid of his ancestors.[6]

When he was nine years old he heard for the first time that he was being called from the spiritual world. He heard it so clearly that he got up and walked out of the tepee. Once outside he saw nothing, but the moment he entered the tepee again he felt a pain in his legs and noticed that something was wrong with him. He didn't enjoy his food any more. The next morning he woke up in pain and his legs would not support him; he fell ill. His hands, legs and face were swollen. He was lying in the tepee and was looking out through the opening to the sky.

Out of the clouds two men came down with the speed of an arrow. They had a spear like lightning in their hands and called, 'Hurry! Come! Your Grandfathers are calling you!' In that moment he was outside his body and entered the invisible world above the clouds, a world of lofty silence. But everywhere around him voices were whispering. In this vision a brown-red horse appeared that spoke to him, 'Behold me! My life-history you shall see.' And then it spoke, 'Your Grandfathers are having a council. These shall take you; so have courage.' The cloud in which he found himself changed into a tepee in which six ancient men were sitting, who were as old as the mountains, as old as the stones. The oldest said to Black Elk, 'Your Grandfathers all over the world are having a council, and they have called you here to teach you.'

The six old men were the Powers of the World, one of the north, one of the south, one of the east, one of the west, one of sky and one of the earth. Black Elk was shaking with fear at this council. But the ancestors gave him a bright red stick that was alive and told him to plant it in the earth. He took the stick and planted it in the earth and a great tree sprouted from it in which many birds had their nests. Under the tree appeared two roads that crossed, a red road from north to south and a black road from east to west, from sunrise to sunset, from life to death. Black Elk was told to walk these roads with his people. The last to appear to him was the oldest, the spirit of the earth who said, 'My boy, have courage, for my power shall be yours, and you shall need it, for your nation on the earth shall have great troubles.'

Then in the vision he was back on earth, saw his village, the horses emaciated, the men and women sick, the children dying. There were only sick and dying people. He was told to plant the stick in the earth in the middle of the village. Again the stick sprouted into a tree; the people were called to life and Black Elk was told to lead his people on the red road.

He walked on the red road and after him came his people. He called his people, and the children and the sick and the dying were brought to life. An innumerable army of the dead walked behind him. And the voice of the spirit of the earth sounded: 'Behold, a good nation walking in a sacred manner in a good land.'

He walked across a green land until the red road crossed the black road that goes from east to west. He did not want to take that road, for it went to the setting sun, but he had to take this road by order of the voice that had given him the task. In the next camping place the stick withered. The birds that had accompanied them disappeared, the faces became skinny and pale, the horses were skin and bones and stumbled. They were walking the way of death, and he knew that his people would lose all the forces they had received from the beginning. But the horse took him alone higher, up to the highest of the mountains. Far below him he still saw his people.

But when he stood on the mountain he saw not only his people, but the entire earth. He saw more than he could say. He understood more than he saw, and he saw the holy circle of his people, taken up in the great circle of all peoples. Together the circles of all those peoples formed one gigantic circle, and in the centre stood a holy tree that protected all creatures. And thus he went back to the earth through the rainbow with the staff of his ancestors in his blood. He saw his people, his village, his tepee, and was back home as a sick boy in his tent.

For twelve days and nights Black Elk lay as dead in his tent before coming back into his earthly consciousness. After this he had the gift of prophecy and the task of leading his people, part of the Sioux Indians, in the knowledge that this people had to go the way of death.

This is a record of a people that had almost died out at the time, and had been forced to walk a tragic path. But even now there are those for which ancestor worship and nature religion are daily realities.

Kofi Edusei wrote a book about the culture of his west African tribe. His story also gives an impression of the tragedy of many nature peoples who, whether they want to or not, have to go through the eye of the needle in order to develop new capacities from within.

Kofi Edusei was the son of a prominent medicine man in Ghana who was told by his father to go in his footsteps and become the leader of the tribe. But Edusei did not do that. He went to school and learned arithmetic, reading and writing. With his learning he lost his clairvoyant capacities. He became a teacher and in that process the way of initiation was closed to him. He obtained a responsible position in Ghana until chaotic conditions in his country forced him to flee. In 1979 he fled to Poland, and from there to Germany where he applied for political asylum. Via all kinds of detours he was invited into a youth group of the Christian Community in Stuttgart where he told his story. Out of this first contact a friendship developed with my colleague Dieter Hornemann.

In his book, Edusei described the venerable culture of Ghana which, on the one hand, lives with the reality of the spiritual world and those who have died, but on the other is threatened by overpopulation, poverty, hunger and the loss of the old clairvoyant capacities and instincts. This loss shows that there is no way back – only forward by developing the intellect and spiritualising intelligence.

In England Kofi Edusei became acquainted with new agricultural methods. Equipped with new insights he was able to return to his people, and now helps them enrich this ancient culture with new capacities.

3

The Patriarchs in the Old Testament

Descriptions of ritual abound in the Old Testament, whereas in the New Testament ritual plays only a minor part. Simply looking at quantities shows a striking difference: in the Old Testament the word 'altar' occurs over 300 times, whereas it appears only 22 times in the New Testament. This simple comparison alone already points to a great difference between the two books.

Christ himself emphasised this difference when he said, 'My concern is what lives in the heart, not the service of sacrifice,' (Matt.9:13) but at the same time he agreed with the religious and ritual order of his time, to the extent that they had not degenerated: 'You should go to the priests and show yourself to them. Make the gift of offering which Moses prescribes, as a proof to them.' (Matt.8:4) Without a doubt Christ spoke here out of the insight that these forms of ritual have value and significance. It is not a concession to ritual tradition, but a confirmation of it. Connecting with the tradition of his time he continued its development. We will repeatedly encounter this principle of continuity and progress in the development of ritual forms.

In the Old Testament we can observe a way from 'outside' to 'inside'. Noah and the patriarchs Abraham, Isaac and Jacob brought their offerings in the open air. In the time of Moses and his successor Joshua, offerings were made in the tabernacle, the tent that was carried on the journey through the desert to the promised land. From that time on the offerings were brought following fixed rules of ritual by ordained priests. Not until Solomon's time did the Jewish ritual become an inner world with the Holy of Holies in the temple as its centre. Christ continued this inward path; 'Where you have gathered a treasure, thither your heart forces will bear you.' (Matt.6:21) Parallel to this way from outside to inside, the animal sacrifice gradually disappeared and was replaced by plants, as well as the offering of soul forces. In this direction we move from the Old Testament to the New Testament.

Ritual comes into being at the time when the creation falls apart; when the human being no longer 'sits in God's lap'. Paradise is a time of 'ligion' (Latin *ligare* means to connect), but not of 're-ligion' (re-connect). Not until God becomes a counterpart, in other words, after the fall into sin when human beings severed themselves from the Creator, does the longing for religion arise. In the first three chapters of Genesis we don't find a trace of ritual – until the moment when the gate of paradise is closed. Only then does the need arise in human beings to connect anew with the Creator.

To be precise, ritual is described for the first time in the Old Testament with Cain and Abel. But the beginning of ritual life on earth carries a certain tragedy. Enigmatically, Cain's offering is not accepted by the Godhead. When you read really carefully you discover that the separation between Cain and Abel developed much earlier already than by the difference in their offerings. Cain is of a different descent than Abel. In the English bible (RSV) Eve says at the birth of Cain, 'I have gotten a man with the help of the LORD' (Gen.4:1). But the original Hebrew text is stronger, 'I have gotten a man from Yahweh.' Cain comes from a union between Eve and Yahweh. To make it even more complicated, Jewish sagas relate that Cain is born from a union of Eve with the archangel Samael.

No matter how you look at it, in all traditions Cain was not a son of Adam. He was of a different descent than Abel, whom it is explicitly stated was a son of Adam and Eve. From the beginning they were an unequal pair of brothers. But they both brought sacrifices. Their ways may remind us of Prometheus and Epimetheus in Greek mythology. Prometheus was the 'precursor'; he stole the fire from heaven. Epimetheus looked back. In any case Cain was in a certain way ahead of his time, whereas Abel lived with the consequences of the fall and offered what Yahweh apparently demanded of the human being.

Among the descendants of Cain were Jabal, Jubal and Tubal-Cain. They brought agriculture, music, technology and iron-work to the earth. Cain was the human being who did not leave the earth to its fate. He cultivated the earth, harvested the fruits of the field and offered those. Cain was in a certain sense born prematurely. He had no concept of good and evil. By his divine origin he was not yet aware of the consequences of the fall, as Abel already was. Abel lived on what the earth gave. He could be called a child of the fall, and was conscious of human shortcomings. As a shepherd Abel wandered with his flocks and offered the first-born of his cattle. His offering corresponded with what Yahweh expected of the human being at that time. This offer was accepted. Animal sacrifice played a crucial role in the countless ritual acts described in the Old Testament. By contrast, for some puzzling inexplicable reason, Cain's offering was rejected.

We have to stop for a moment and consider animal sacrifice and its importance, not only in the Old Testament, but in all pre-Christian cultures. What is this strange need to bring blood sacrifices and burn them in fire and smoke? When we try to imagine the nature and constitution of Old Testament people in our minds, it is not difficult to picture that the sight of the animal sacrifice must have evoked many things in the human being. In us it already awakens emotions. But in antiquity the impression was infinitely more profound. In those times people could not just stand there and look at it without being moved; their inner world, even their physiology, participated in the outer observation. People's own blood followed as it were the movement of the offering. The outer event of the offering called up willingness to sacrifice and surrender, so that the outer sacrifice was accompanied by the human soul.

Ever since the earliest civilisations humanity was divided between farmers and shepherds, the ones who cultivated the earth and those who connected themselves with the animal world. The biblical term for this is sons of man and sons of God. Abel was a son of man with earthly parents. In a certain way, Cain was a son of God, as we have seen. Their ways were vastly different. Cain was cursed and exiled, and had to wander east of Eden. Only after a long time did these two separate streams connect with each other again, namely when the time was fulfilled at the birth of Jesus. Jesus Christ was the one who united the Son of God and the Son of Man for the first time. In a certain sense he again brought the offering of the world of plants, Cain's sacrifice, in the form of bread and wine.

First, however, these two streams in ritual moved apart and did not come together. With the birth of Seth the stream of Abel was continued. Eve said at his birth, 'God has appointed for me another child instead of Abel.' When Seth also had a son, religious life became visible on earth: 'At that time men began to call upon the name of the LORD' (Gen.4:25f). This is when ritual came into being, not only in the form of sacrifices, but also in the form of the liturgical word. This motif, which is connected with Abel (we will come back to Cain later), can be followed throughout the Old Testament. A large part of the Old Testament describes how ritual developed in this Abel stream.

The first sacrifice we encounter after this is the burnt offering that Noah made to the Lord after the Great Flood had subsided. Noah built an altar and offered of the clean cattle and clean birds. The Lord then spoke anew the words, 'Be fruitful and multiply, and fill the earth' (Gen.9:1). But now it was an answer to the human being who from then on lived in the midst of trials: sowing and harvesting, cold and heat, summer and winter, day and night. The Lord also answered with a covenant that he established with humanity and all living beings; he promised that there would not be another all-destructive flood. The sign of this covenant was the rainbow, a visible sign in the sky. It is noteworthy that the rainbow does not so much remind human beings of the covenant as it reminds God himself.

Step by step we can follow the development further with the three patriarchs, Abraham, Isaac and Jacob who, each in his own way, erected altars. Together they built seven altars.[1] The number is undoubtedly not arbitrary. Each of them built an altar in an unusual place. Now we can remind ourselves of Chapter 1 about the Stone Age, in which places were described where stone monuments were erected more than 5000 years ago. Even today these places emanate a strong radiance that is experienced by countless people. They are 'power spots'. Clairvoyants can also perceive that in the aura of these locations. For such places the Hebrew language uses a powerful word, *maqom,* 'sanctified place' or 'foundation place'. Again and again we find this word for the places where the patriarchs built their altars. These were not arbitrary spots. The patriarchs walked their paths faultlessly and recognised the peculiar potential of the landscape.

They were able to continue what their pagan predecessors, the Canaanites, left behind.

Rites and ritual grow in exceptional places. We witness it everywhere on earth. In China we have feng shui, the knowledge of wind and water, the capacity to perceive from wind, water and soil condition where the earth has a particular vitality. Taoism has chi, places on earth where chi, life force, is concentrated. In northern Europe there are the dolmen, menhirs and other stone monuments – everywhere we find a similar principle. Rituals come into being in places where in a certain sense heaven touches the earth, where the spiritual world is near. Spiritual human beings in antiquity were able to perceive where ritual had to be performed on earth. Abraham did not need to use a divining rod; he followed God's voice when first he travelled through the promised land after he had come from Ur of the Chaldeans.

The sacrifices of Abraham

'Abram passed through the land to the place at Shechem, to the oak of Moreh. At that time the Canaanites were in the land. Then the LORD appeared to Abram and said, "To your descendants I will give this land." So he built there an altar to the LORD, who had appeared to him.' (Gen.12:6f).

Abraham looked in all four directions when he stood in a high place and looked over the promised land. By order of Yahweh he walked the land in its full length. He did not go like a sleepwalker straight to the place where he had to be, but he first explored the land. As he walked he tested the earth in a certain sense. It was a search for a sacred spot, until he found the *maqom* at Shechem and at the oak of Moreh.

Long before the Old Testament people reached the promised land, the oak already had a particular significance. The Hebrew name of the tree is *elah* which is related to *el,* the word for God. The tree of God. The inhabitants of Canaan celebrated their rituals at this sacred tree before Abraham and his company arrived there, because they also recognised it as a power spot. The name Moreh means something like the voice of an oracle. These are signs of a pre-Jewish religion that reminds us of old nature religions. It is noteworthy that Abraham did not eradicate this old religion root and branch, but went along with these pagan forms of ritual, with this oracle – there was no hostile takeover, no trace of force. The new land was not conquered by fire and sword, but was annexed without a struggle. And in complete harmony with what existed already Abraham added his altar to this sacred place. 'So he built there an altar to the LORD, who had appeared to him.'

In the shade of the oak, in the ambience of this tree he experienced the presence of the Godhead; this was a consecrated spot with a sacred tree. It was a place where heaven was open and Yahweh revealed himself to Abraham. In a certain sense many people today can identify with this. For this reason old power spots are often visited and more people than ever are interested in them. At the same time, however, the opposite is also happening; consciousness of such exceptional places seems to disappear. Hordes of tourists and photographers certainly don't make it easy, for example, to say a quiet prayer in the Cathedral of Chartres. But the principle still holds that there are select places on earth which, if they are cultivated, can be dwelling places for the divine world. The real problems begin when such places are neglected or desecrated. A *maqom* is a spot where the human being can, in the true sense of the word, come home, to themself and to God:

> So Abram moved his tent, and came and dwelt by the oaks of Mamre, which are at Hebron; and there he built an altar to the LORD (Gen.13:18).

Here developed a second ritual spot. The historian Josephus reported even in the first century after Christ that there was a sacred oak near Hebron. Abraham stayed at the oaks of Mamre for some time. This place was decisive for one of the most important events described in the Old Testament, the encounter of Abraham with Melchizedek.

From Hebron Abraham travelled to the Valley of the Kings which tradition says is the Kidron Valley near Jerusalem. There he met the priest-king Melchizedek. Very briefly the Old Testament indicates that Melchizedek stood higher than the patriarch, that his God was higher than the God of Abraham. He was priest of El-Elyon, God Most High. Abraham made an offering to him and Melchizedek blessed him.

> And Melchizedek, king of Salem, brought out bread and wine; he was priest of God Most High. And he blessed him and said, 'Blessed be Abram by God Most High, maker of heaven and earth; and blessed be God Most High, who has delivered your enemies into your hand!' And Abram gave him a tenth of everything. (Gen.14:18–20).

In a significant way the New Testament mentions Melchizedek again in the letter to the Hebrews, which was written out of Jewish tradition. The letter was written for Jewish priests, the Hebrews, who had turned from Judaism to Christianity. The unknown author of this letter saw himself faced with the task of explaining the difference between the Jewish and Christian rituals. This unknown person who, according to Rudolf Steiner belonged to the school of John the Evangelist, wrote:

> This Melchizedek of whom we are speaking is king of Salem, the priest of the highest God. He went out to meet Abraham who was returning from the war of the kings. He blessed Abraham, and Abraham gave him a tenth of all that he possessed. His name when translated means, firstly, king of righteousness, and then he is also called king of Salem, that means king of peace. He is without father, without mother and without ancestors, without beginning of days or end of life: he is of similar nature as the Son of God and he is a bearer of priesthood for ever. Imagine how great he must be that Abraham, our patriarch, sacrificed a tenth of all the spoils of war as an offering to him! (Heb.7:1–4).

This timeless figure, who united priesthood and kingship in himself, has become a likeness of the Son of God. He approached Abraham with bread and wine. For the first time the two offering streams met again: Abraham, the Hebrew – as he is called for the first time in this part of the Old Testament – the representative of the

Jewish stream that worshipped Yahweh, one of the seven Elohim, and facing him Melchizedek, priest of God Most High. The one brought an animal sacrifice, the other offered bread and wine. Subsequently Melchizedek disappeared without a trace and only returned in the description in the Letter to the Hebrews. Only in one psalm do we hear a short sentence that is spoken to the Messiah: 'You are a priest for ever after the order of Melchizedek' (Ps.110:4).

The Old Testament shows the development from the animal blood sacrifice to plant offering. This plant offering was the beginning of an inner offering, which we cultivate even today, for instance, in the Act of Consecration of Man: 'We all draw near to you in soul, O Christ, that you offer us with you...' That is the readiness to sacrifice that is right for our time, connected with the offering of bread and wine on the altar. The offering of Melchizedek is practised in Christendom even today.

A mosaic in the church of San Vitale in Ravenna, Italy, shows two offerings facing each other at one altar. In this mosaic the two ritual movements of pre-Christian humanity are represented. We might

Figure 4. The offerings by Abel and Melchizedek, San Vitale, Ravenna.

expect Cain and Abel, but the artist pictured Abel and Melchizedek. To the left of the altar stands Abel who lifts the lamb, the first-born of his flock, up to the altar. On the right stands Melchizedek with the consecrated bread in his hand that reminds us of the plant offering. Thus the two approach the altar of the Highest God. The offering of Melchizedek is confirmed by Christ. Of Christ himself it is said, 'Thou art a priest for ever, after the order of Melchizedek' (Heb.5:6). God himself says this to Christ. This priesthood, which unites the two, is bestowed on Christ.

> Abraham planted a tamarisk tree in Beer-sheba, and called there
> on the name of the LORD, the Everlasting God (Gen.21:33).

After the covenant with Melchizedek the Lord also entered into a covenant with Abraham, who until then was called Abram. He received a new name, Abraham, and he was promised numerous descendants and a new land. Then, after the birth of Isaac, Abraham placed his tents and his altar under the trees. In Beer-sheba (seven springs), where he entered into an agreement with army commander Abimelech, he planted a tamarisk. For Abraham the presence of the tree was the basis of his offerings.

The sacrifice of Isaac

God said, 'Take your son, your only son Isaac, whom you love, and go to the land of Moriah, and offer him there as a burnt offering upon one of the mountains of which I shall tell you' (Gen.22:2).

Two thousand years before Christ, when Abraham turned in inner quiet to God, he received the inspiration to go to the mountain Yahweh would show him. There he received the order, 'Take your son, your only son Isaac ... and offer him as a burnt offering.' There is not a word in the Old Testament about what stirs in Abraham's soul when he received this inspiration. For us it would be reason for profound psychological explorations to describe what all was moving in him when he received the order to sacrifice his son, his only one. But Abraham was silent. It is as if he accepted the impossible order without question.

We find a similar kind of acceptance in the well-known words, 'The LORD gave, and the LORD has taken away; blessed be the name of the LORD' (Job 1:21). How difficult it is to speak these words with conviction in critical moments is something I experienced myself when our first child died after three days. Only after years of mourning was I able to make these words my own. Maybe this inadequate analogy shows the kind of surrender Abraham must have had to obey the order. Abraham walked with his son for three days. 'On the third day Abraham lifted up his eyes and saw the place afar off.' Here the word *maqom* appears again. And although Abraham had not been to this place before, he recognised it. After all, Yahweh had told him of the place, 'the mountain that I will show you.'

'On the third day Abraham lifted up his eyes.' Did he walk for three days without looking up? We could imagine that he walked in a mood of inspiration. In the three days during which he walked together with his son, he listened inwardly for the inspirations from Yahweh. The holy place to which Yahweh directed him was Mount Moriah, the same mountain on which King Solomon later built the temple.

What did Abraham see when he recognised this spot, which was revealed to him by the divine world? Undoubtedly he perceived something of the aura of the place. In anthroposophy we have the concept of 'etheric geography'; the etheric world, the world of life forces, which works differently in different places on the earth. Clairvoyants and initiates can recognise and name the qualities of etheric forces. In the colours of the aura the initiate recognises what has been engraved on this spot. Again, Abraham recognised the spot 'from afar'. He left his ass and his servants behind, and walked alone with his son, his only child, to the spot that would later be called the Temple Mount.

These are sober words, evidence of a muted drama. To the question of his son, Abraham replied only, 'God will provide himself the lamb for a burnt offering, my son.' His readiness to sacrifice was tested to the extreme, until at the last moment the angel intervened and called a halt. A ram caught in a thicket by his horns could take the place of the child. Then Yahweh said, 'because you have done this, and have not withheld your son, your only son, I will indeed bless you' (Gen.22:16f).

Through the centuries the relationship has been recognised between this pre-Christian offering and the sacrifice that took place on Golgotha two thousand year later: God offered his only Son. But here, in the sacrifice of Abraham, we find preeminently the origin of the Jewish ritual, the temple ritual. A long way leads from the sacrifice of Abraham to the countless offerings that were brought in the tabernacle and the Holy of Holies in the temple of Solomon.

Isaac, the son of Abraham, had connections with other places. He celebrated the ritual in places where water flowed, at springs and wells, where he experienced the Godhead in flowing water: El-Olam, God of eternity, of the eons, of cycles of time. Thus Isaac dwelt at Beer-Lahai-Roi, the well of living and seeing. By his own experience he was connected with the mystery of life and death. And in a certain sense he was a seeing seer although his eyes failed him in his old age, as a result of which others could deceive him. He recognised the wells his father had dug and that had been destroyed by the Philistines; he restored them and gave them the same names they had in his father's time. Then he dug another three wells, Esek, Sitnah and Rehoboth, after which he went back to Beer-sheba where he had spent his childhood.

Both for Isaac and his son Jacob, religious experience of the day changed into divine revelation by night. At Beer-sheba Yahweh revealed himself to Isaac during the night. When Isaac woke up the next morning he knew that he had to build an altar in this place. The revelation was followed by the offering. His son Jacob did the reverse when he came to Beer-sheba years later. When Jacob was already an old man, a patriarch, he travelled by Beer-sheba on his way to Egypt. There he brought an offering to the God of his father in broad daylight. In the following night Yahweh revealed Himself to him. 'Then he said, "I am God, the God of your father; do not be afraid to go down to Egypt, for I will make you a great nation".' (Gen.46:3). As a reply to the offering God bestowed the prospect of his future on him, the future of the people of Israel.

Even today the relation of day and night is an important element in ritual acts. The evening before a service at the altar is the best time to prepare for the act. What is more or less consciously received at the altar is unconsciously and supra-consciously worked through during the subsequent night. In this mysterious process of waking and sleeping, of consciously taking in and unconsciously working through, the actual miracle of the altar service takes place.

The offerings of Jacob

Finally, Jacob, the third of the patriarchs, had a particular relationship to stones. He erected stones as altars in a few places. In the following passage the word *maqom* is used three times.

> And he came to a certain place, and stayed there that night,
> because the sun had set. Taking one of the stones of the place,
> he put it under his head and lay down in that place to sleep.
> (Gen.28:11).

In this sacred place he saw heaven opened in a dream. As he woke up, this nightly revelation was continued in a ritual. Jacob said, 'How awesome is this place! This is none other than the house of God, and this is the gate of heaven.' He set up a stone, anointed it with oil – a ritual act – and called the place Beth-El, House of God. Later in life he returned to this spot. Again God appeared to him in the night and Jacob received a new name, Israel, a name that came with a promise for all his descendants, the Jewish people. Again, Jacob erected a stone that he anointed with oil (Gen.35:6).

This was now the way that defined the entire further history of the Jewish people, namely to build a house for God on earth, a Beth-El. The true task of the Jewish people was to build a dwelling place, a temple for God on earth. In a literal sense that was the temple of Solomon. In the figurative sense it was the preparation of the coming of the Messiah. After the coming of Christ the motif of temple building became an inward one: 'And the Word became flesh and lived among us' (John 1:14). And the crowning goal of the long road is the New Jerusalem, 'See, the dwelling of God among men!' the Book of Revelation says of this image of the future (Rev.21:3). God has connected himself again with humanity.

4

Jewish Ritual and the Temple of Solomon

The temple of Solomon has a long history leading up to it, which goes back all the way to the patriarchs. It began with the sacred places (*maqom*) that are decisive for the oldest ritual forms of the Jewish people. For the temple of Solomon was also build on such a spot, Mount Moriah, where Abraham was to sacrifice his son Isaac, as described in the previous chapter. The endeavour for building the temple, and the temple rites, were closely connected with Moses. In his life the great sacred place was Mount Horeb in Sinai, the mountain where he was called by God.

Here burned a spiritual fire that spoke, 'I AM WHO I AM' (Exod.3:14). It was Yahweh who would lead humanity like a shepherd to a new future, to the coming of the Messiah. This took place in a time when for the Egyptians the gods had fallen silent: Osiris, the sun god, was dead and Isis had remained behind as a widow. Humanity was waiting to see what the gods would do and what would happen on earth.[1] Yahweh then told Moses that, by means of ten plagues, he would force Pharaoh, the ruler of Egypt, to let the Hebrew people go. In Egypt also the Passover festival was instituted, the feast of the Passover lamb, the unleavened bread and the bitter herbs – for bitter was the lot the Jewish people were leaving behind. The Hebrews ate the meal standing up, ready to depart to the promised land. At the time this festival was instituted the Hebrews were also instructed to celebrate it every year anew:

> This day shall be for you a memorial day, and you shall keep it as a feast to the LORD; throughout your generations you shall observe it as an ordinance for ever ... And you shall observe the feast of unleavened bread, for on this very day I brought your hosts out of the land of Egypt. (Exod.12:14,17).

Thus in the time of Christ, and even now, the Jews celebrate this feast in springtime to remember the exodus from the land of oppression,* the journey through the desert and the arrival in the promised land. In the time when the temple was standing in Jerusalem (First Temple 660–585 BC, Second Temple 515 BC – AD 70) the Passover lamb was offered and eaten there. After the destruction of the temple, the Passover lamb was no longer eaten; Passover then became the feast of unleavened bread. Today it has the character of a family feast, the Passover Seder, that is celebrated at a table. Passover was also the basis of the Last Supper that Christ had with his disciples.

After the exodus from Egypt, Moses received on Mount Horeb the assignment to make a tent that would serve as a temple, the tabernacle. At the same time a priestly line of descent was ordained: Moses' brother Aaron, his sons and descendants would be priests in the tabernacle, and later in the temple. All priests serving in the temple were from the tribe of Levi. On the mountain in Sinai, Moses also received the ritual and liturgical instructions for the priests and the Jewish people. The tabernacle was carried with the people through the desert and Canaan. It was only later, at the time of Solomon, transformed into the temple.

The form of the temple

It is a long search into history, but also into secret knowledge in antiquity, to discover where the temple had its origin. We find one point of access with Agrippa von Nettesheim (1486–1535), a medieval Rosicrucian who derived the symbolism of the temple from the human body:

> The human being, as the most beautiful and most perfect work of God, as his likeness and as a world in miniature, has the most perfect and harmonious stature of all creatures, and contains in him all numbers, measures, weights, movements, elements, in brief, everything belonging to his completion ... For this reason, people in antiquity, who counted on their

* The Hebrew name of Egypt, *Mizraim,* means tribulations.

fingers and expressed numbers with their fingers, seemed to prove that all numbers, measures, proportions and harmonies were derived from the members of the human body. On the basis of the composition of the human body, therefore, they also created their temples and other works of art. Yes, God himself taught Noah to build his ark in accordance with the measurements of the human body.[2]

In antiquity it was known that the human body was the norm for everything that was built on earth, from the moment Noah built his ark. Ancient tradition tells us that Noah, by an inspiration for the measurements of the ark he received from the Godhead, built the ark after human measurements. Those old traditions tell of a line running from Noah's ark via the tabernacle to the temple of Solomon: all three were built after human measurements.

Figure 5 shows the proportions of the tabernacle and the human body; the proportions are important, not the measures. The human being lying down with arms outstretched relates to the length of the tabernacle, while when he sits up, his head touches the top. The tabernacle was an image of the human being stretched out. We also find it in other pre-Christian cultures. The human body was a reflection of the goddess of heaven – the Egyptian Nut – who conceived the human being out of the divine plan. When the human being died, he went back, according to Egyptian tradition, to 'the measure of Nut'. Several Egyptian Pharaohs had images on the inside of their sarcophagi of the goddess of heaven Nut with her arms stretched up; she is surrounded by stars (Figure 6). The human body again forms part of its divine origin.

Figure 5. Proportions of the tabernacle and the human body.

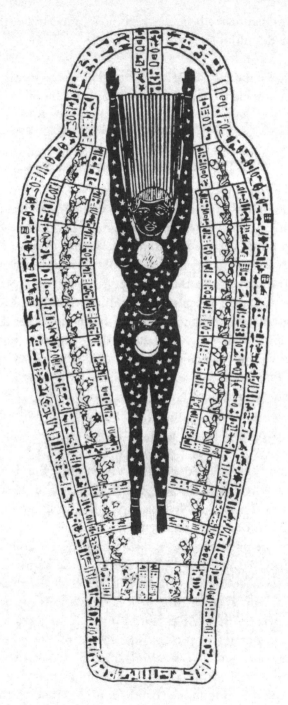

Figure 6. The Goddess Nut pictured on a sarcophagus.

Rudolf Steiner described the relationship between the human body and the ark of Noah as follows:

> If we imagine the human being enclosed by those forms which his ether body has to have so that the form of the physical body is built in the right way, then we arrive at the measurements of the ark of Noah. Why does the Bible give the size of the ark of Noah as 50 cubits wide, 30 cubits high and 300 cubits long? Because these are the proportions which human beings have to have in the transition from Atlantean to Post-Atlantean times, so that the right thought forms will be shaped, which is the reason why the length, width and height of the bodies of Post-Atlantean human beings were built in the right way. In Noah's ark we have a symbol of the proportions of our present bodies. These measurements are the effects of those thought forms that Noah experienced, and that he built into the ark in such a way that, by beholding these forms, the thought world arose on the basis of which the organism of Post-Atlantean humanity would be formed. Humanity was educated through effective symbols. The proportions of our physical body today are the proportions of the ark of Noah. If the human being stretches his arms upward, we have in the proportions of Noah's ark the proportions of the human being today.[3]

The human being condenses out of the world before birth into the proportions as they existed in the ark of Noah, and thus incarnates into a physical body. The ark of Noah and the tabernacle both had human measurements; they both expressed the architecture of the physical body. Even more precisely than in Noah's ark we can follow how this form was conceived in Moses' inspiration for the architecture of the tabernacle. The tabernacle was no arbitrary structure, but was a spiritual archetype that Moses saw. Most English translations of the Bible use the word 'pattern'. When Moses was inspired to inaugurate the Jewish rites, every imagination – the spiritual image of the tabernacle, the altar, the shewbread, etc. – was accompanied by the words of Yahweh: 'And see that you make them after the pattern for them, which is being shown you on the mountain' (Exod.25:40). Down to the smallest details, these rites followed their spiritual archetypes.

We can be even more precise: from what were these forms of ritual derived? They were pictures of the macrocosm. The tabernacle was a microcosmic temple. Moses beheld how the macrocosm can be manifested in the microcosm in accordance with the ancient principle: as above, so below. In Genesis, the first book of the Bible, we find the same wording at the creation as was used for the 'genesis' of the Jewish rites. At the creation we find the following expressions, 'Thus the heavens and the earth were finished, and all the host of them.' After the rest on the seventh day the text continues, 'So God blessed the seventh day and hallowed it, because on it God rested from all his work which he had done in creation' (Gen.2:1,3).

We find when the tabernacle was completed, 'Thus all the work of the tabernacle of the tent of meeting was finished' (Exod.39:32). Then follows a description of all the ritual objects, and the text concludes with the words, 'And Moses saw all the work, and behold, they had done it; as the LORD had commanded, so had they done it. And Moses blessed them' (Exod.39:43). Here Moses became a co-creator. In the construction of the tabernacle the development of the creation was reflected in sevenfold form. Rudolf Frieling was the first to call attention to the sevenfold correspondence.[4]

Briefly summarised, we recognise the following correspondences:

- The *first* day of creation: heaven and earth were created. The first revelation of the tabernacle: Moses was told to erect pillars and stretch a tent over them. Thus the picture of heaven and earth was reflected.
- On the *second* day the Godhead separated the waters above the firmament from the waters under the firmament. There is a mysterious border area in the heavenly spheres where the waters below were separated from the waters above. It is an invisible boundary line that separates the spiritual world from the visible heavenly and earthly world. The second instruction Yahweh gave Moses for building the tabernacle was the separation of the Sanctuary from the Holy of Holies. The Sanctuary was the world where the human being was still in the realm of visibility, the place where the priest brought the offerings; but this world was separated from the Holy of Holies by a curtain.

- The *third* day of creation: the earth was clothed in a green covering of plants, 'yielding seed' and 'bearing fruit'. The third image for the tabernacle was the twelve shewbreads, which were the gift of the world of plants.
- On the *fourth* day of creation the heavenly lights were placed in the firmament. Moses was told to make a seven-branch lamp stand, a perfect expression of the correspondence between the divine creation and the creation of ritual on earth.
- The *fifth* day of creation: the lower animals were created. Moses received the task to build the altar for scented offerings. With incense human beings offer to the Godhead their soul forces, their astral forces (which are akin to the animal kingdom).
- On the *sixth* day the higher animals and the human being were created. Now Moses was told to build the altar for burnt offerings. This was not for the incense offering (from plants), but animal sacrifices.
- On the *seventh* day nothing happened in an outer sense; God rested on the Sabbath. For Moses this was the moment when he was told to make the laver in which the priest washed his hands. In washing his hands the priest left everyday reality behind so that he could fully dedicate himself to the sacred. In silence the divine in human beings can become active. Herbert Hahn, one of the very first Waldorf School teachers, wrote, 'When I am truly still, God works in me.' That is a fitting expression for the seventh day. Rest on the Sabbath does not mean that you do nothing. Originally it was the day on which human beings became still, so that the Godhead could come to manifestation in them, through them.

From here it is but a small step to the temple of Solomon. Solomon doubled the measurements of the tabernacle on the same ground plan: the forecourt, the Sanctuary and the Holy of Holies. He had the intuition that this temple could stand in no other place than Mount Moriah where – according to Jewish tradition – the foundation stone of creation lies, where the creation has its foundation.

The tabernacle (Figure 7) consisted of a tent with the laver in the left foreground, and the altar in the centre. The space was threefold: the forecourt, the Sanctuary and the Holy of Holies.

The temple of Solomon (Figure 8, over page) had a forecourt with the two pillars, Jachin and Boaz, a long central part (the Sanctuary) and a rise to the Holy of Holies that was built in the form of a cube. The temple was not large: 60 cubits is about 30 metres (100 ft), the width was 20 cubits (about 10 m, 35 ft), and the height 30 cubits (1 Kings 6:2). It was a simple, small temple. Emil Bock wrote:

> The Temple of Solomon did not possess any outer magnificence and beauty: its forms were plain in the extreme, its dimensions unpretentious. If we go by the specifications of the Bible, we arrive at a picture of a rectangular external structure lacking any significant divisions and ornamentation.[5]

Both the tabernacle and the temple of Solomon grew out of the proportions of Noah's ark. But in the transition from the tabernacle to the temple we not only witness a larger scale; the temple also incorporated a new symbolism. This symbolism not only pointed to the origin of creation, like the tabernacle: the human body as the 'temple of God.' Now, in a remarkable interplay between Jewish and pagan elements, a new symbolism arose in the history of temple construction.

Figure 7. The tabernacle.

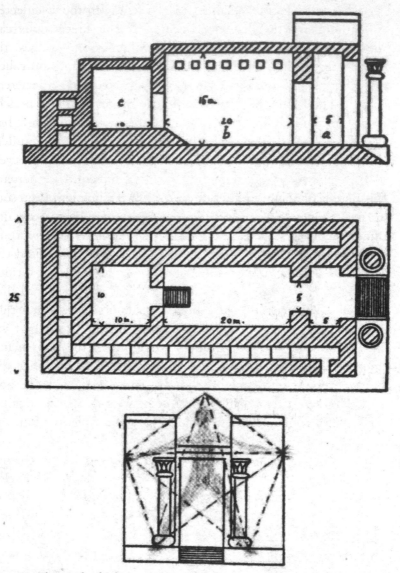

Figure 8. The temple of Solomon.

The Jewish temple cannot be compared with Greek or Egyptian temples. Solomon built a Messianic temple, a temple in which Christ could recognise himself so that he could say, 'Demolish this temple, and in three days I will raise it up anew.' No one understood what he said, but the evangelist added, 'he was speaking of the temple of his body' (John.2:19,21).

The symbolism of the temple of Solomon is even today reflected in the construction of the Masonic lodges. The Freemasons call their place of assembly the 'temple of Solomon'. Some lodges still come together in Israel at the high points of the year, in the so-called Quarry of Solomon (Zedekiah's Cave), to celebrate their rites there.

Of old, people knew the temple of Solomon to be a perfect representation of the human being, not as he was in the past, but as he will become in the distant future and has become manifest in Jesus Christ. Philo of Alexandria, Thomas Aquinas and even Luther still knew that the threefold form of forecourt, Sanctuary and Holy of Holies was a reflection of the human being's body, soul and spirit. The passage from soul to spirit was covered by a curtain. When someone enters the realm of the spiritual world, a curtain opens. Even today we recognise in experiences on the threshold the picture of the curtain. For example, someone who during a serious pneumonia crossed the threshold to the spiritual world, related that a moveable 'wall' before him became transparent like a curtain that dissolved. Behind it appeared a heavenly landscape with souls of the departed whom he recognised. At that point the curtain closed again, it became cloudy until a new wall formed itself – and he heard the words, 'Not yet.' Then he returned into his body.

In the middle area, the soul realm of the temple, stood the altar for the burnt offerings. There something ignites and lights up in the human soul. The seven-branch menorah and the twelve shew-breads stood there, images of the sevenfold and twelvefold human being. They expressed cosmic images (as in the seven planets and twelve signs of the zodiac).

In other pre-Christian rites we also find indications of the cosmos that was reflected on earth. In Roman times the priests called the chasuble (the colourful priestly vestment) *planeta*. In the colours of the course of the year the chasuble expressed the mood of the cosmos, the mood of the planets.

In a number of temples we find a distinction between the Sanctuary and the Holy of Holies. A curtain or gate marked the separation. In antiquity the appearance and composition of the curtain was an image of the four elements, which separate the visible from the invisible world. When someone enters the spiritual world, they first experience these elements as spiritual beings, as I describe in my book, *Lord of the Elements*.

The curtain in the temple of Solomon was made of four different substances which were expressions of these elements. In antiquity byssus, white linen, represented the earth element; the purple part expressed the element of water;* the hyacinth-coloured part symbolised air, and the scarlet part fire. These were symbolic indications of the way leading from the visible to the spiritual world. Thomas Aquinas viewed the curtain as a prophetic indication of the coming of the Messiah, who would enable the human being to step from the realm of the soul into the realm of the spirit. Or as Rudolf Steiner said, 'The temple – that is the human being who receives the spirit in his soul.'[6] Ritual makes it possible for human beings to receive the spirit in their soul. In the Christian Community this is spoken to the children when they enter the church for the Children's Service in the words, 'You know you are going to the service that will/is to[†] lift up your soul to the spirit of the world.'

The temple of Solomon was at the same time a foreshadowing of the death and resurrection of the Messiah. This was the reason why he could say, 'Demolish this temple, and in three days I will raise it up anew.' At the moment the Crucified One died, the curtain of the temple was torn in two from top to bottom. His martyrdom made the separation between the two worlds dissolve. But also the destruction of the temple in AD 70 was confirmation of this prophecy.

At the dedication of the temple, Solomon spoke the words, 'The LORD has said that he would dwell in thick darkness. I have built thee an exalted house, a place for thee to dwell in for ever.' (2Chr.6:1f). Naturally, pious Jews knew that the Godhead had himself decorated heaven with stars, that he had placed the sun in the firmament, but that was not the essence of their experience of faith. In Judaism people had to take the inward path so as to prepare their body for the coming of the Messiah. This is the reason why the way into the temple of Solomon led to a part where it was completely dark. Outside in the forecourt the world was visible. The Sanctuary was a dimly lit world. The Holy of Holies was literally invisible. It was the destiny of the Jewish people to close the eyes and become all ear.

---

* Purple, a very precious colour that was reserved for kings and cardinals, was made from the murex sea snail, which secretes a tiny drop of purple.

† There are some small differences in translation between the wording in Britain and in other English-speaking countries.

This is confirmed in the Old Testament commandment, 'You shall not make for yourself a graven image' (Exod.20:4).

In the foregoing we established that the temple is firstly an image of the coming of the Messiah. With the insights of this chapter we can take another step. For not only the coming of the Messiah, but also his resurrection, and even the future of humanity are visibly symbolised in the form of the temple. What Christ brought to realisation is something that all human beings can bring on the path of imitation. 'Do you not know that you are a temple of God and that the Spirit of God would live in you?' (1Cor.3:16).

Ever since Christ, the motif of temple building has been transformed into an inner act. The ultimate goal of this long road is the New Jerusalem. In the future spiritualised creation, the external temple and ritual service will no longer be needed: 'A temple I did not see in the city. The Lord, the divine ruler of all, is HIMSELF its temple together with the Lamb.' (Rev.21:22).

Ritual and the psalms

Of the prayers that were said in the temple nothing much has been preserved. We do know what kinds of offerings were made: food offerings, burnt offerings (animal sacrifices), incense offerings, morning and evening offerings. Psalm 141, for instance, reads: 'Let my prayer be counted as incense before thee, and the lifting up of my hands as an evening sacrifice!' In the first part of the Old Testament, the Law of Moses, many of these offerings are described and prescribed. Several of the psalms contain prayers and descriptions of ritual acts. This gives us a picture of how the temple was regarded, what took place there and how faith was viewed by the Jews at the time.

Many words in the psalms that describe the rituals occur also in later Christian liturgies.[7] Some examples:

'The blessing of the LORD be upon you! We bless you in the name of the LORD!' (Ps.129:8) These words were transformed into the blessing in the Latin mass: *Dominus vobiscum,* the Lord be with you.

'Let my prayer be counted as incense before thee, and the lifting up of my hands as an evening sacrifice! Set a guard over my mouth,

O LORD, keep watch over the door of my lips!' (Psalm 141:2f).[8] In the Latin mass this text from the psalm is spoken in the offertory *(Dirigatur, Domine, oratio mea, sicut incensum, in conspectu tuo … Pone, Domine, custodiam ori meo, et ostium circumstantiae labiis meis).*

'I wash my hands in innocence, and go about thy altar, O LORD' (Psalm 26:6). In the Latin mass of the Mozarabic or Hispanic rite the priest washed his hands after the offering and spoke this psalm text *(Lavabo inter innocentes manus meas et circumdabo altare tuum Domine).*

But many psalms are also sung in their entirety, sometimes as the response of the congregation to the reading of the Gospel, sometimes during the communion. In some traditions, all 150 psalms are said within a specific period of time, and are then repeated. Thus the psalms become a guide for the soul.

The Greek temple

Greek culture shows the opposite of Jewish tradition. Whereas in Judaism the way leads inward ('You shall not make for yourself a graven image'), Greek culture leads the human being outward to the visible world of images.

The temple was constructed in a decagon into which the human being did not fit; but stood outside it. The symbolism of the Jewish temple did not apply here. There was no ark, chest or tabernacle in the temple that symbolised human proportions. The Greek temple was built in complete harmony with the landscape. In the Greek theatre, which proceeded from the temple rites, we see a similar connection. Greek theatre was not limited to the stage, but pulled all of surrounding nature into the drama. Thus for instance, the sea might have been used as a backdrop out of which the actors sailed onto the stage.

The Greek temple did contain a *cella* in its centre, a closed space where the cult statue of the Godhead stood. Just as in the Jewish temple, this was the domain into which only the high priest entered. But around it there was a completely different world. Everyone could freely enter and walk about in it. Also the non-initiated Greek could ascend the temple steps and walk among the columns, the peripatetic way, the walking way. Everywhere you could see the landscape between the columns. The temple was embedded in the landscape.

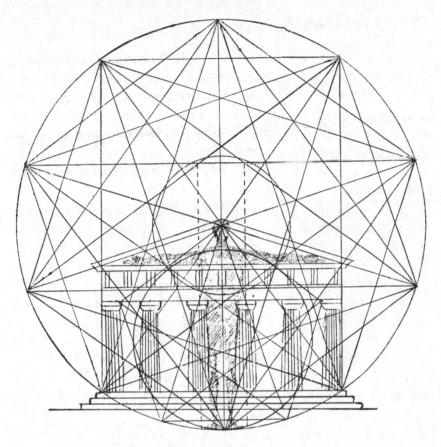

Figure 9. The Greek temple and the human body.

Even the offering was embedded in the landscape, for in the Greek temple service the offering was brought outside the temple. Here perfect harmony reigned between the inner and the outer world in which one could walk about.

It has been said that the Greek temple was built on two contrasting principles: on the one hand the principle of the Holy of Holies, on the other hand that of a stone monument. The columns represented the standing stones. Two totally opposite principles which, on the one hand lead to an inner world, the Holy of Holies, but on the other hand also point to the outer world. In the little town of Thermos, for instance, a temple of Apollo stands. A rectangular *cella,* in which the statue of Apollo was kept, is surrounded by 36 columns placed in an oval – the principle of a stone monument.[9]

The Temple Legend

After this contrast we return to the temple of Solomon. The building of this temple required a most unusual collaboration between two cultures. Although in Solomon's time Israel was strongly opposed to all cultures around it, King Solomon called on a master builder from pagan Tyre. Hiram 'was full of wisdom, understanding, and skill, for making any work in bronze' (1Kings 7:14).

According to ancient tradition, the King of Tyre called the master builder Hiram his spiritual father. It was most unusual for a king to call a master builder his spiritual father. The Old Testament says of Hiram that he was the 'son of a widow'. We know this term from antiquity, among others from the Egyptian mysteries and the Greek Adonis cult.[10] It is the indication that a human being went 'through the eye of the needle', became poor in spirit, 'son of a widow', in order to receive resurrection wisdom in his poverty. In the Egyptian mysteries a person who had gone this path was called a 'son of Isis'.

In Jewish tradition the story of Cain had a sequel that referred to the building of the temple. One of Cain's sons, Tubal-Cain, became 'the forger of all instruments of bronze and iron' (Gen.4:22). According to spiritual tradition, Hiram was a descendant of Tubal-Cain. He thus stood in the lineage of Cain.

There is a marked contrast between Solomon and Hiram. Solomon was not a son of Cain, but of Abel. The name Solomon means 'bearer of peace'. He did not gain this peace through his own trials and initiation, but it was bestowed on him as grace. Solomon was the human being who had developed the future part of our being, manas, spirit man. Again, two age-old cultures that were estranged from each other clashed. Cain and Abel – history repeats itself.

We can read about this antithesis in the Old Testament and in Jewish traditions. There is also another document that gives insight into the symbolism of the temple of Solomon, the Temple Legend. The origin of this legend is unknown. In the period between 1500 and 1725 it appeared in printed form in a number of alternative readings. More than a hundred manuscripts from that time have been preserved. It is thought that the Temple Legend originated among the builders of the French cathedrals in the Middle Ages.

The legend describes in greater detail than was indicated above how Cain and Abel came from different worlds and it relates that one of the seven Elohim united with Eve, which resulted in the birth of Cain. Abel was born from the union of Adam with Eve. Cain was a son of a god; Abel a son of a man. By their two different kinds of offerings a conflict arose caused by the jealousy of Yahweh. Yahweh himself brought about the conflict between Cain and Abel. Cain was not a descendant of Yahweh but of one of the other six Elohim.

Old Jewish tradition spoke of the existence of seven Elohim. Just as among the Greek gods there was conflict and strife, among the seven Elohim there was also jealousy. The analogy holds in so far that both Greek and Jewish tradition speak of high angel beings who reflected the highest Godhead, but not of the Godhead himself. We saw this distinction earlier in the encounter of Abraham with Melchizedek. Abraham worshipped Yahweh; Melchizedek was priest of the God Most High, El-Elyon. The Elohim were divine beings of the rank of the Exousiai. The jealousy of Yahweh was aroused by the fact that Cain and his sons made creations of their own, for Jabal, Jubal and Tubal-Cain were the inventors of the arts of building, music and metalwork.

After Cain's death, this family in a certain sense led its own life. One of the descendants in the time of King Solomon was the master builder Adoniram, also called Hiram. Hiram received the task from God to form an army of free men. They had to bring about a connection between the sons of fire (the Cainites) and the sons of man (the Abelites), in order that these groups could henceforward live in peace with each other. Hiram was chosen by Solomon to be the master builder of the temple. Initially it looked as if a perfect collaboration grew between King Solomon and his master builder. But at some point a third person became enmeshed in the collaboration.

From the Old Testament we know how the Queen of Sheba, Balkis, visited King Solomon (2Chr.9). The Temple Legend relates that Solomon asked her to marry him, and she consented. When the temple was being built Queen Balkis wanted not just to see the building but also wanted to meet the master builder. As if he sensed what this meeting would lead to, Solomon at first denied her request. But as she kept insisting, in the end he could not resist. The moment Balkis looked at Hiram, it was love at first sight. Solomon was consumed by jealousy.

Three journeymen who had been rejected by Hiram because they were not initiated in the secrets of temple building became Solomon's henchmen. They were at odds with Hiram and concocted a plot to cause his work to fail. The greatest work, the casting of the bronze sea, still had to be accomplished. This was a ritual object that stood in the forecourt of the temple. It was a gigantic bronze casting with twelve bulls that carried a basin on their backs.

What was the meaning of this symbol? Twelve bulls, twelve primal powers underlying creation carried a basin in which was kept the water for ritual washing. It was a prophetic picture of the future divine incarnation, the picture of the Son of Man who unites all primal powers, and who becomes the vehicle, the bearer of the Son of God – Jesus becomes the vehicle of the Christ. The sea of bronze was a Messianic symbol that did not stand hidden in the temple, but was visible to everyone in the forecourt. It was the skilful son of Cain, Hiram, who worked the metal for this, but then things went wrong.

During the casting of the work of art the three journeymen interfered and caused the work to fail. The red-hot mass of metal flowed through the temple. Hiram tried to save what he could and poured water on the hot bronze, but this then exploded and Hiram was pulled into the depths by the sea of fire. There he was initiated into the secrets of the earth. His forefather, Tubal-Cain, led him to the centre of the earth where Cain dwelled. Cain put a hammer (the ancient Tao symbol) into his hands with which he ascended again out of the depths. With this magical object he could still complete the sea of bronze. However, the three journeymen killed Hiram by order of Solomon. Thus the old fratricide was settled. Cain had slain Abel; now Solomon, son of Adam, avenged the fratricide on Hiram, son of Cain, in accordance with the old principle of an eye for an eye and a tooth for a tooth. However, this did not prevent Hiram from having added a new aspect to Jewish tradition.

One of the elements that are new for Jewish temple symbolism is the picture of the two pillars Jachin and Boaz, that were placed before the entrance to the temple. It was a pagan symbol that we also find in the Egyptian temples. These two pillars were standing free, without carrying a roof or arch. The sound of the two names alone already indicated a world of difference. Jachin was the pillar of day; the name consists of bright vowels and consonants. Boaz, the pillar of night has dark vowels and consonants. Day and night, life and death – a Jew entered the temple through this symbol. This image also contained a prophecy. A time would come when between the extremes of light and dark, day and night, life and death, a third would come who could say of himself, 'I am the door.' Only then would the symbolism of the two pillars have found its fulfilment.

The question remains, however, how the ways of Cain and Abel will ever come together. Here, according to Rudolf Steiner, an important task lies for anthroposophy, the task to unite these two contrasting streams. But this takes us to a controversial realm.

In his little book, Hans Peter van Manen goes further. On the basis of a fragment from Rudolf Steiner he described anthroposophy as the Cain stream and the religious way as the Abel stream. The one stream works into the physical world and builds out of its own forces; the sons of Abel live out of receptivity, out of grace. Although Van Manen usually expressed himself more subtly, here he did the opposite. He put certain value judgments on the streams of the sons of Cain and Abel, based on a poem by Marie Steiner that she wrote in 1927 in memory of Rudolf Steiner. It begins with the words:

> You are not like pious worshippers,
> Who wander silently about, unworldly:
> In flames your spirit created, purging worlds
> Raising them from ignominy's depths ...[11]

Even if it is true that Marie Steiner made a value judgment on 'pious, unworldly worshippers' (it is well-known that she initially held herself aloof from the Christian Community), in fairness we must quote her revised view of the relationship of anthroposophy and the Christian Community. On 5 November, 1948, a few weeks before her death, she wrote a letter to her good friend, Wilhelm Salewski, one of the founders of the Christian Community:

> In the long run this cannot last. The two movements will
> have to find each other again. They may exist side by side for
> thirty years and mutually explore their possibilities, but they

will have to come together. (That is the answer I have to give myself when I try to put myself in the spirit of Steiner. For he did not want dogma, but life) ... I think we have to seek for ways of blending.[12]

The view that the contrast between the Cain and Abel streams must at all cost remain is, in my opinion, no longer of this time. Although there are indeed people who live out of this one-sidedness, the reality is usually that we need both qualities to make progress in life: activity *and* receptivity. Hella Wiesberger also came to the conclusion that it is our task to overcome the antithesis between Cain and Abel both in the individual human being and in humanity in general.[13]

Rudolf Steiner made consistent efforts to bring these opposing streams, that threatened to evoke conflict and jealousy, together. He said in one of his esoteric lectures, 'I have reserved for myself the aim of bringing about a reconciliation between the race of Abel and those of the race of Cain.'[14] The reconciliation between Cain and Abel can ultimately come about in human beings wherever we succeed in creating harmony between the one-sidedness of activity and of receptivity. Art, religion and science cannot become productive until their productivity is preceded by moments of quiet receptivity and inspiration. A perfect balance between the two poles is voiced by Herbert Hahn whom I quoted earlier:

> When I am truly still,
> God works in me.

But the picture is not complete without the next sentence:

> When I truly work
> I rest in him.

5

Mithraism

The French theologian Ernest Renan (1823–92) once made the drastic statement, 'If some mortal disease would have prevented the development of Christianity, the world would have embraced Mithraism.' And in the works of a contemporary of Mithraism, the early Church Father Tertullian (*c.* 160–220), we read, 'In the Mithraic service the demons ape the holy acts of Christianity.'

That is sufficient reason to want to trace the content of the Mithraic religion, and find the differences and resemblances with early Christianity. The symbolism of the Mithraic religion was so similar to that of Christianity that one can become confused. Was Mithraism a form of Christianity before the time, or was Christianity a continuation of the Mithraic religion?

The two share a certain kinship, not only in form but also in content. For Mithra is announced as 'the Coming One', he who would restrain and overcome the bull. He who would go before the human being as leader of the soul *(psychopompos)* in life and death. He who would die and return to life, would raise the dead, and in the last struggle would overcome evil. Afterward he would lead his followers to a new world, a new heaven and a new earth. It must have been shocking for early Christians to hear this from another religion, one that was being contested and opposed!

Mithra the mediator

The origin of the Mithraic religion is unknown, but in the ancient Indian Rig Veda, and ancient Persian writings of the Yashts we already find indications pointing to Mithra. As is often the case, these documents were preceded by oral traditions. We must in any case go back to the ancient Indian and ancient Persian cultural epochs to find traces of the origin. For instance, we read in Yasht 10:

Mithra we worship, who possesses the broad fields. Who as spiritual Yazata rises over the Hara Mountains, ahead of the immortal sun with the fast steeds; he, the first to mount the glorious heights adorned in golden twilight; from there he commands all the lands ... the strong hero.[1]

In these documents Mithra is the mediator between the great sun god Ahura Mazda (or Ormuzd) and humanity. His name indicates that he is a mediator. The word *mi* means covenant, agreement; the suffix *thra* means causing, doing. Mithra then means he who brings about the union (between heaven and earth), the mediating power. He was called the greatest victor among the gods. He was therefore not a human being, but a divine being. Originally Mithra was an angel being. Because of his mediating role he belonged to the Persian *Yazatas,* which had the rank of (sun) archangels. Referring to this, Rudolf Steiner said that Mithra was the divine mediator between the highest Godhead and the human soul.

The Greek philosopher Plutarch *(c.* 46–120) related that the Persians imagined the throne of Ahura Mazda to be at double the distance from the earth to the sun, dwelling as high above the sun as the earth is below it. It is the highest sphere of the Godhead. In the depths of the underworld dwells the opposing power Angra Mainyu (or Ahriman).

Between the highest Godhead Ahura Mazdao and Angra Mainyu stood Mithra, the mediator. That is also how he is depicted (Figure 10). Mithra was born out of the earth and stands in the midst of the twelve signs of the zodiac, forming the centre between the earth and the cosmos. With his right hand he reaches up to the stars, in his left hand he holds a globe, the earth. He stands between heaven and earth, between spirit and matter, and connects the two with a sovereign gesture.

However, for the followers of Mithra this was not earthly reality, but a prophecy. One day Mithra was to be born in a cave in midwinter. He would be surrounded by the four gods of the winds standing in the four corners beside the circle. Three animals, the raven, the serpent and the dog would be watching and worshipping Mithra. The entire realm between heaven and earth is represented in this simple picture, below by the three animals, above by the cosmos, and in between by Mithra.

Figure 10. Mithra as mediator.

Mithraic temples in the Roman Empire

From India, Persia, Asia Minor and via the pirates of Cilicia (southern Turkey), Mithraism came to Rome. In AD 67 a group of Cilician pirates was captured and enslaved. They brought this unknown religion with them. As always, Rome was fascinated by religion. Roman culture hardly had any gods of its own, but a lot of imports. Every god known in the Roman Empire had a place in the Pantheon in Rome.

But there was something exceptional in this new religion. The image of Mithra standing as a warrior between the world of light and the world of darkness, appealed especially to Roman soldiers and army commanders. The merchants who followed in the wake of the army also adopted Mithraism. Everywhere in Europe where the Roman legions went, Mithraism found fertile ground. By the third century Mithraism reached from India to Britain, and from Spain to the Black Sea. At the time there was no other religion that had spread as far and existed for as long as the Mithraic mysteries. In the fourth century virtually all large seaports in Europe had a Mithraeum (Mithraic temple), a subterranean ritual space. All over Europe there are still remains of 441 Mithraea.[2]

These Mithraea were always built as man-made subterranean caves. They all had a round arched roof that was painted with stars. Frequently Mithra himself was represented with a cloak of stars, as an indication of a cosmic being. Usually the sun and the moon were shown beside him. This symbolism by itself shows a movement that stands in contrast to that of the druid mysteries. The druids built their sanctuaries outside in nature, and were completely cosmos-oriented in their ritual observations. We find their oldest stone monuments in places with 'four seasons a day,' as the English will say. In one single day rain and sunshine alternate continually. The druid mysteries could be found in places where nature is strongly present.

The Mithraic mysteries literally closed themselves off from nature and the outside world. They went underground. Outer sunlight played no role any more. The cosmos was imitated in miniature. There are Mithraea in which the positions of the stars were painted on the arched vault the way they were hundreds of years ago. For instance, in the Mithreum in Ponza, Italy the night sky from AD 212 is shown.

Figure 11. Mithraeum.

All Mithraea were built in the vicinity of springs or rivers. If there was no spring or river, a canal was dug, and if this was not possible, a great water basin was built, for water was needed for the ritual. Animal blood sacrifices were made on Mithraic altars. Along the sides of every Mithraeum there were wide spaces for meals of bread and wine, at which wine and water were mixed in the chalice, a ritual custom that found its way into the Christian rites. In the New Testament we find indications of this at the wedding in Cana, where water was changed into wine. But the Christian tradition also has a link to the testimony of John who testified after the crucifixion: 'But one of the soldiers thrust a lance in his side, and at once blood and water flowed out' (John 19:34). The Mithraic religion shows that this imagery is even older. The idea is a union of the personal (wine, blood) with the supra-personal (water).

Eradication by Christianity

In the year 324, Emperor Constantine the Great, who declared Christianity to be the state religion, prohibited all forms of pagan sacrifices. By his decree all rituals were abolished. There was a brief revival under one of the subsequent emperors, Julian the Apostate (reigned 361–63), who rejected the decree promulgated by Constantine, but after him the renewal took hold. The new state Christianity proceeded rigorously and eradicated all traces of pre-Christian mysteries. Although the Mithraic religion spread at the same time as early Christianity, the Christians completely destroyed anything pagan. Under Patriarch Theophilus of Alexandria the library, where all works from antiquity were collected, was destroyed in 391. Thousands of book scrolls were burned. We can hardly make a picture for ourselves of all the pre-Christian mystery streams, because most of the ancient documents were destroyed.

Rudolf Steiner had radical views on this development, saying:

> It would be scarcely possible to imagine a greater contrast than the contrast between the spirit of the early Church Fathers and that of the teachers of the Christian Church and the decrees of the Councils ...
>
> All the terrible measures associated with this destructive work of are very often glossed over like many other things. But this should not happen; for where the truth is sullied in any way the path to Christ Jesus is also obscured and cannot be found.[3]

Destructive forces in state Christianity eradicated essential elements of early Christianity and pre-Christian mysteries and, in so doing, have done great injustice to reality, even though the Mithraic mysteries existed well before Christianity. The Roman Catholic mass also shares similarities with the Mithraic ritual, as is apparent from the statement by Tertullian quoted above. We will elaborate on this in Chapter 6. Ever since excavations made in the 1950s, we know that even the Vatican is built on top of a Mithraeum. Constantine, who built a church on this spot, made every effort to wipe out as many traces of the old sanctuary as possible. Whichever way we look at it, we have to come to the conclusion that both early Christianity and the Mithraic religion draw in part from the same source.

The similarities in symbolism become visible in a few aspects. Of course, both in Mithraism and in Christianity the altar had a central position. The altar as the centre of ritual dates from long before either of these religions. In the mysteries of antiquity the altar was simultaneously a tomb and the place of sacrifice. Also in early Christendom the altar was actually still a tomb. This made a profound impression on me when I visited a number of old churches and monasteries in Georgia and Russia in the 1980s. The monastery of the Holy Trinity and Saint Sergei in Kiev has several altars in which the body of the saint is entombed. In Georgia, I visited a church where the saint was also buried in the altar. As an expression of devotion, visitors of the church went down some steps under the altar and walked up again on the other side. Such forms of devotion were also known in pre-Christian sanctuaries.

When Rudolf Steiner gave indications for the new ritual to the first priests of the Christian Community, he described the altar as 'a tomb in the form of a table'. The form of the tomb has to be visible, and on it a table top. Of course it is no tomb in the literal sense of the word, but the image had to be evoked.

We find the symbolism of the sun and the moon both in Mithraic and Roman Catholic ritual. Mithra is usually depicted with the sun and the moon on either side. We are familiar with similar depictions of the crucifixion: Christ between sun and moon. The picture of sun and moon also appears in the symbolism of the mass, in the Most Blessed Sacrament, in which the consecrated host is held up (Figure 12, over page). The host is surrounded by a golden aureole like a sun with the sickle of the moon underneath. (In the picture the round host is not shown.)

In Mithraism there was a prophecy that one day, in the middle of the winter, Mithra would be born on earth in a cave. Shepherds would come to worship him. The day of this birth, Mithrakana, was 25 December. In the third century after Christ, under the influence of the Roman emperors, this festival day was also called *Dies Natalis Solis Invicti,* the Day of the Birth of the Invincible Sun. For in their eyes, Mithra was identified with *Sol Invictus,* the sun god. In the fourth century the Christmas festival was moved from 6 January

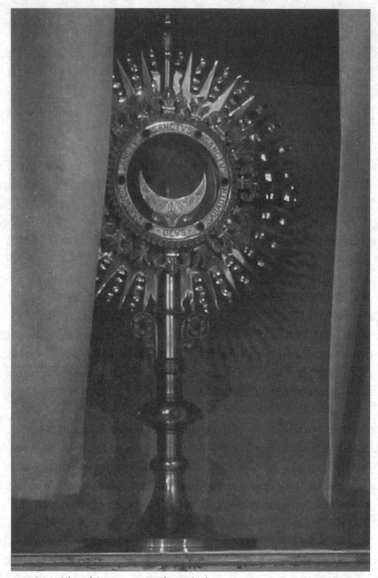

Figure 12. Most Blessed Sacrament without the host.

(when it had always been celebrated) to 25 December because of the Mithraic mysteries.

On the day of Mithra's birth, the darkest time of the year, at midnight, participants in the Mithraic mysteries were told to 'behold the sun at midnight' – thus sounds the classical expression for initiation. For this reason, once a year the mass was celebrated at midnight on 25 December, the darkest time of the year, a custom continued until today.

We can still find Mithraic initiates depicted in a fifth-century fresco in Ravenna, Italy, of the adoration of the Christ child. The kings are not wearing crowns but Phrygian hats, a sign of Mithraic initiation. We could continue to list of such parallels almost endlessly.

The Mithraic mysteries

But there are historians who, in my view, are shortsighted when they assert that Christianity is a replica of the Mithraic mysteries. Early Christians felt differently about that. Justin Martyr (105–166), for instance, turned it around and said, 'Before the birth of Jesus Christ there were Christians already; only they didn't use that name.' He also wrote, 'The creative Word that made all things, the Logos, was already working before Christ.' We also know this from the Gospel of St John (1:1,3): 'In the very beginning was the Word, ... All things came into being through him.' Early Christians said that the Word lives in miniature in every human being as the *logos spermatikos,* as a germ, a seed. In some people it expresses itself strongly. Early Christians viewed Socrates and Heraclitus as precursors who lived in harmony with the Logos, and were in their pagan existence yet 'Christians before the time'. This is how the best representatives of early Christianity regarded these pre-Christian mysteries.

It is most interesting to trace not only the similarities, but also the differences. According to some Church Fathers the difference consists primarily in the fact that pre-Christian religions were foreshadowings of the coming of the Messiah, and that with his coming the old prophecies were fulfilled.

However, in the Mithraea we also find ritual symbolism that is far removed from Christianity. For the central event in the ritual is the sacrifice of a bull. This has been depicted in countless images. Mithra is shown at the moment when he subdues the bull, taking it by the horns. He almost always appears between two torchbearers (Figure 13, over page). Usually the torchbearer Cautes stands on the left pointing his torch down, while on the right stands Cautopates with his torch pointing up. (In Figure 13 both torches are pointed down.)

Figure 13. The sacrifice of the bull. Relief in Vatican Museum, Rome.

Fire pointed down symbolises death, and the upright torch symbolises new life. Mithra standing in between shows the way from death to new life. The torchbearers are always depicted with their legs crossed. They stand on the side as if they have no part in the fight but are mere witnesses. Their position with crossed legs is an expression of keeping a distance.

Between the torchbearers the figure of the god Mithra appears, usually sitting on the bull while he kills it with a dagger. A dog and a serpent drink the blood of the bull. Ears of wheat grow from the tail of the dying bull. Sometimes there is even an ear of wheat in the flowing blood. The animal life that is offered and dies brings forth higher life. It is not an earthly but a cosmic image. Mithra is surrounded by seven stars. Above and below him there are seven fire altars, and among them in the upper row are seven trees. Sun and moon stand on either side and below is a scorpion stinging the bull's genitals.

Rudolf Steiner explained this picture as a duality that lives in every human being. Each person has two beings within that contend for mastery: a higher and a lower being. The human being stands between animal and cosmos, as Mithra is placed between bull and cosmos.

The higher human being has the task of subduing the lower one, keeping it under control. If that does not happen, says the imagery of the Mithraic mysteries, then the animal forces become dominant and in the end even destructive – the image of the poisonous scorpion. If the lower human being is left to his fate, he will cripple himself. If unbridled passions lead a life of their own, they eventually become destructive. That is the imagery of this path of self-knowledge. It is the battle of the spirit against nature, of human consciousness against animal instinct.

After the bull has been killed, continues the legend, Mithra receives the sign of his victory. He kneels before Helios, the sun god, who hands him his aura. The radiance of the sun pales at this victory by Mithra. From that moment Mithra becomes *Sol Invictus,* the invincible sun. He has a festive meal with Helios. This meal of bread and wine was probably also shared in the Mithraea. When the victory is won, the god Aion appears and a new cycle of time begins. The word eon was derived from the name Aion.

At the end of a cycle Mithra appears as Aion, the youthful god of time (Figure 14, over page). In antiquity before the Ancient Persian culture, time was pictured as a serpent biting its own tail: everything repeats itself. The eternal return of the same is the oldest representation of time. In Persia, however, time was shown differently, as a serpent spiralling up around the human body and raising its head upwards.

In the Act of Consecration of Man the term 'cycles of time' is used. At a certain point, time is rounded off; a time span has then ended. In the dynamic forms of religion this does not mean an eternal return to the same (as in 'there is nothing new under the sun'), but continuance on a higher plane. This is pictured in the image of the serpent that winds its way up around the body.

Mithra is here shown with wings. In one hand he holds a bunch of lightning rods, in the other the staff as the sign of the royal power of the I. He stands on a strange shape that is pictured above his head in mirror image, as if he has just come out of an egg and still has the eggshell below and above him. It is the image of the world out of which he is born. The sickle of the moon stands behind his shoulders. He is surrounded by the signs of the zodiac and by Aion. In the extreme corners are the four gods of the winds.

Figure 14. Mithra as Aion. Museum Modena, Rome.

Everywhere Mithra is announced as the Coming One, but nowhere in the myths and images does his birth appear as a human being on earth. That lies in the future. Mithra is a being who descends step by step, eon by eon, from cycle of time to cycle of time – the divine mediator. Rudolf Steiner explained, 'The cult of Mithras was something like a final, powerful recollection of the Christ still not yet arrived on Earth, but descending.'[4] That is the essential difference between Christianity and Mithraism. But the human being who went through these Mithraic mysteries and in the spirit saw this divine being descending could, step by step, overcome their own bull nature and enter into communion with the higher worlds.

Initiation in the Mithraic mysteries

The Mithraic mysteries had seven degrees of initiation. A cursory review of these initiation degrees shows that aspirants had the task to free themselves more and more from their bull nature, in order to be able to enter into a supra-personal community with the divine world. That was the task of the Mithraic initiation. Rudolf Steiner added, 'Thus the whole purpose of these mysteries lay in establishing ceremonies and rituals that could bring the neophyte in contact with the spirits who had for the most part died long, or even very long, ago.'[5]

- The *first* initiation stage was that of *corax,* the raven. Aspirants received the task to mediate between the earthly and the spiritual world, just as the raven goes back and forth like a messenger. More concretely, they had to mediate between the physical world and that of the dead. We find the same imagery in the king of the mountain legend of Emperor Frederick Barbarossa who is not dead but asleep in a cave in a mountain. The legend says that every day ravens came to tell the dead emperor what was happening in the world. At this first stage, the aspirants had to learn to think with the thoughts of the dead, and thus mediate between the worlds of the living and the dead.

- Concerning the *second* stage scholars are not fully in agreement. Rudolf Steiner called this stage the *occult one,* the hidden one. Aspirants had to be silent and listen, and thus learn the language of the dead. These days the term 'occult one' is used by scholars for all phases of initiation, and this specific phase is called *nymphus,* the bridegroom. For at this stage the aspirants vowed to be faithful to the mysteries. But essentially, it was a stage in which one learned to be silent, as we know from all mysteries.
- In the *third* stage the movement was reversed. After the silence the aspirants became *miles,* a fighter. They had to apply what they had learned during initiation to the outer world. They were sent out into the world.
- The *fourth* stage was called *leo,* the lion. Rudolf Steiner used a different term and spoke of the *sphinx* (which, of course, also contains the lion). In this phase the aspirants not only had to listen to another language, but also had to learn to speak another language, a language of imagery or a language of riddles, as the sphinx does.
- In the three highest stages the aspirants had to overcome their own bull nature. In the *fifth* stage they became *Perses,* a Persian, a representative of a whole people. We recognise a similar indication in the New Testament when Jesus said of Nathanael, 'an Israelite in whom there is no untruth' (John 1:47). At the stage where the aspirants became one with their people and became a Persian or an Israelite, they became a carrier of a higher being. The archangel of the people was able to read their soul, so that they were not only a mediator between the living and the dead, but also between humans and hierarchies.
- In the *sixth* phase of the initiation the aspirants became *heliodromos,* sun runner. The human 'I' had become so great, so at one with the cosmos, that it beheld the sun at midnight and encountered in the sun the Coming One, the Messiah.
- In the *seventh* stage they became *pater,* or even *pater patrum,* father of fathers. Now they had not only become one with the sun, but with the world of the Father, and could become part of a new creation, as announced in the Apocalypse: 'He who overcomes, I will grant him to sit on the throne with me,

as I, too, have won the victory of the spirit and sit on the throne with my Father' (Rev.3:21). 'Sitting on the throne' with the Godhead means participating in the future creation as co-creator and father.

To a certain extent we can still recognise the seven initiation phases in the seven orders of the Roman Catholic Church, as these existed until 1973. The first four orders were called the minor orders:

- *ostiarius* (doorkeeper, sexton – a clear relationship with *corax,* raven)
- *lector* (reader of the Bible)
- acolyte (server at the mass)
- exorcist (clear connection with *leo/sphinx*)
- subdeacon
- deacon and
- priest

The original word for priest, Greek *presbyteros,* actually means the elder, and can therefore be compared with the initiation term Father. Finally, the bishop has the so-called 'fullness of the office', and can celebrate all seven sacraments. The original Greek word for bishop is *episkopos,* overseer, someone who oversees a large area.

Thus in our explorations we find in the Mithraic mysteries for the first time a number of noteworthy parallels with Christian rituals. Even in the gospels we can read descriptions of events that were celebrated identically in the Mithraic religion. When Christ was tortured on Good Friday he underwent trials that also took place in the Mithraic mysteries: the aspirant had to undergo a scourging, was then clothed in a royal robe with a sceptre and received a crown of thorns of the acanthus plant. The Gospel of Matthew (27:29) uses the same word for the crown of thorns (acanthus) as in the Mithraic mysteries.

6

The Origin of the Christian Ritual

The Last Supper

It is generally regarded as self-evident in Christian circles that the Christian ritual has its origin in the Last Supper on Maundy Thursday. But in the foregoing chapters we have seen that elements from pre-Christian mystery streams also underlie this ritual. The Eucharist is not based solely on the Last Supper, as some denominations assert. It is worth looking at the origins of the mass in its early forms.

Christianity, and therefore also the Christian ritual, justifies itself on the life of Jesus Christ. In a certain sense, Christ Jesus' whole life after his baptism in the Jordan was a ritual celebration. Sometimes the apostle Paul also used the inversion of the two names, so as to make clear that ever since the baptism Christ had become the 'principal person'. The human being Jesus became the bearer of the Christ, and thus the Son of God. He dedicated the life he led to the people and to the Father God who sent him to the earth. Because of this the deeds he performed on earth received the value of sacramental acts. For the divine dwelt and worked among us on earth. These deeds would acquire great importance for the later Eucharist. Think of the marriage in Cana, where water was changed into wine – a prelude to the transubstantiation at the Last Supper. Think of the feeding of the four thousand and of the five thousand, for which the physical substances of bread and fish were transformed. But also the Transfiguration on the mountain has the character of a ritual, for Christ himself was transfigured. In the transformation of his earthly appearance he brought his true being to manifestation.[1]

This stream is joined by the prayer the Christ taught his disciples and of which he was the living example. They asked, 'Lord, teach us to pray.' The question was answered with the Lord's Prayer. With this prayer the bridge was built between heaven and earth. The realm of the divine could reach the world of earth again. For this reason it would later, in the altar sacrament, mark the transition from the transubstantiation to the communion. The Lord's Prayer is read after the bread and wine are transubstantiated and before they are given in the communion, and go out into the world through the people. With the Lord's Prayer we cross a threshold; a conversation can take place anew between God and human being. Speaking to the founders of the Christian Community Rudolf Steiner called the Lord's Prayer a 'dialogue with the Divine'.

Ritual and prayer culminate in the Last Supper when the Passover was celebrated in an upper room on Mount Zion. Christ himself was the Passover lamb. It is the archetypal image of the community (the twelve and the one) connected by love. In early Christianity *agapē* (spiritual love) was the expression for the Eucharist. Thus shortly before the death on the cross, the Last Supper became an indispensable step toward the Eucharist. For this reason, the priest always speaks the words Jesus spoke over the bread and the wine before he gave them to the disciples. In Rite One of the Episcopal Church the text is:

For in the night in which he was betrayed, he took bread;
and when he had given thanks, he brake it, and gave it to his
disciples, saying: 'Take, eat, this is my Body, which is given for
you. Do this in remembrance of me.'
    Likewise, after supper, he took the cup; and when he had
given thanks, he gave it to them, saying: 'Drink ye all of this;
for this is my Blood of the New Testament, which is shed for
you, and for many, for the remission of sins. Do this, as oft as
you shall drink it, in remembrance of me.'

The words end in the assignment, 'Do this in remembrance of me.' In Greek the word *anamnēse* is used which means more than our everyday memory. When Plato used this word in his philosophy, he indicated the capacity to call up the pre-birth world of ideas. When we take the word re-member literally – bring what once was inward to life and make it a member of our being again – we approach what Christ meant with the word *anamnēse*. It is not about a memory of facts, formulations or ritual acts, but about evoking his presence through Christianised remembering.

But the text and the act of the Last Supper do not suffice to understand what happens thereafter in the Eucharist. After the Resurrection there are several indications in the Bible that point to a continuation of what began there. The event of Emmaus, where Christ revealed himself after breaking the bread, was a sequel to the sacred meal. And Luke wrote about the time until the Ascension: 'By many manifestations of his being he had shown himself as the victor over death after his passion. For forty days he revealed himself to their seeing souls and spoke to them of the mysteries of the Kingdom of God.' (Acts 1:3). In these forty days the Resurrected One appeared repeatedly in the circle of the eleven disciples in the closed space of the cenacle, the upper room, and spoke to them. A famous Coptic document from early Christianity, the Pistis Sophia, describes in enigmatic pictures the 'secret teaching' of the Risen Christ in this period. Both the Greek and the Russian Orthodox Churches consider the forty days as the time when the altar sacrament came into being.

St Jerome is the source of a tradition that at this time James, the brother of Jesus, received the task to celebrate the Christian altar sacrament for the first time. He related:

'Bring a table and bread,' said the Lord ... He brought bread
and blessed and broke and gave to James the Just and said to
him, 'my brother eat your bread, for the Son of Man is risen
from among those that sleep.'[2]

Other traditions add that, following Christ's directions, James called the disciples together and offered them the sacred meal, as the Resurrected One himself had done in their circle earlier. James therefore was the first to have celebrated Holy Mass.[3] From this moment began what in Christian theology is called the 'ubiquity' of Christ: through the Ascension he is 'omnipresent', wherever his meal is celebrated on earth.

Even after this, the formation process of the Eucharist was not yet complete. In a certain sense this was only the beginning, for starting with Pentecost the sacred act came out of the world of the Resurrected One into the world of human beings. The Acts of the Apostles relate that the people now had the meal themselves. 'And devoutly they tended the teachings of the apostles, the celebration of communion, the breaking of bread and the prayers ... They tended the breaking of bread from house to house and received the gift with rejoicing and inwardness of heart.' (Acts 2:42,46).

The expression 'the breaking of the bread' is the oldest name of the Eucharist. When breaking the bread, Christ revealed himself in Emmaus. Also in the feeding of the five thousand this is an important part of the act: 'He took the five loaves and the two fish, lifted up his soul to the Spirit, blessed and broke the loaves' (Mark 6:41). When the bread is broken, spiritual forces can stream into the opened physical substance. It is in a certain sense the distinctive mark of Christ's meal. For this reason the act is performed at the altar even today.

For clairvoyant perception, the aura of Christ appears at this moment as a halo of golden radiance around the consecrated host, or as a golden cloud over the altar. Starting with Pentecost the earthly history of the Eucharist also began to develop in the community of Christians who together formed the *ecclesia,* the church. But the *ecclesia* is inconceivable without a long history leading up to it, namely the pre-Christian mysteries, the Nativity, the Baptism in the Jordan, the feeding of the four thousand and of the five thousand, the Transfiguration, the Last Supper, the Crucifixion, Easter, the Ascension. All the prior events of the life of Jesus Christ are connected with this meal.

But also in the other sacraments the life of Christ on earth lives on. In the imagery of the Middle Ages, for instance, the relationship of the events on Golgotha with the seven sacraments was shown (Baptism, Confirmation, Mass, Confession, Last Anointing, Ordination and Marriage). In old paintings we can sometimes see that the blood from the wound in the side of the Crucified One is caught in seven vessels that symbolise the seven sacraments (for instance in the Frisian Museum, Leeuwarden, Netherlands). This imagery goes back to St Augustine's commentary on the Gospel of St John: 'from his side, pierced with the spear, as he hung on the cross, that the sacraments of the Church flowed forth ... The sacraments are the vessels of grace and of the merits of Christ.'[4]

The Eucharist and the mysteries

Less familiar is the relationship of the Eucharist to the old mysteries. We may surmise some elements from what we know about the Mithraic mysteries. And on two occasions Rudolf Steiner pointed to this relationship. On 17 March, 1905 he gave a lecture at the request of Mathilde Scholl in Cologne about the significance of the mass. What was virtually new for the time in this lecture is the statement that the mass has its roots in pre-Christian mysteries. In her summary of this lecture Mathilde Scholl wrote:

> If we want to learn what the origin is of the Catholic mass,
> we have to go back in time to the mysteries. Mysteries were
> places of ritual where higher wisdom was not only taught and
> acquired, but relevant content was also demonstrated. In the
> religious streams from Egypt and Persia the mysteries adopted
> a popular form. Out of these the mass has developed.[5]

In another lecture series Rudolf Steiner expressed it with more precision:

> What, fundamentally, is the inner significance of the Catholic
> Mass? What is it? The Mass, together with everything associated
> with it, is a contining development of the Mithras mysteries
> combined, in a certain sense, with elements from the Eleusinian
> Mysteries. It is none other than the continuation of ancient
> rituals.[6]

This formulation has a certain one-sidedness, even though it was good to bring this aspect to the fore since it had been underexposed until then. In this regard, it is important to know that the mysteries of Eleusis had a strong connection with life, death and resurrection. In addition, here also the birth of a divine child of whom salvation was expected, played a big role.

A year after these lectures the Benedictine Odo Casel published a book about the Roman Catholic mass. He made a connection between the mass and ancient mysteries. Casel noted that early Christianity adopted a variety of expressions from the Hellenistic mysteries and used them in the sacraments. The concept of 'mystery' is of central importance in Casel's work, as well as the idea that in the act of remembering the reality of historical events is evoked. Only at the second Vatican Council (1965) did the Roman Catholic Church acknowledge this view.

The one-sidedness of this view, which highlights one specific aspect of the mass, was balanced by Rudolf Steiner in a lecture in which he described the working of the risen Christ in the development of the altar sacrament:

> The Mass is a wonderful emulation of the four stages of mystery initiation, and its adoption can be traced back to the teachings imparted by the Risen One to the disciples who were capable of grasping their higher, esoteric meaning.[7]

On the one hand, this formulation follows the tradition of early Christianity, in which the teachings of the Risen One were central. On the other hand, something important is added about the form of the mass. For people who are familiar with the Roman Catholic mass it is in our day not at all self-evident that this ritual consists of 'four stages of mystery initiation'. The fourfoldness itself of the mass is not easy to recognise, since in the course of time all kinds of parts were added to the original form. In the usual conception a distinction was made between the Liturgy of the Word (preparation, Psalm reading, Gospel reading and the Creed) and the Liturgy of the Eucharist (offering, hand washing, intercessory prayer, consecration, Lord's Prayer, communion, thanksgiving, dismissal). Steiner described four parts – gospel reading, offertory, transubstantiation and communion – which are the 'emulation of the four stages of mystery initiation'. Elsewhere Steiner described what he meant with the four stages of the classical initiation. In a lecture in 1913 he named the four stages as follows:[8]

1. To come into the vicinity of death
2. Experiencing the elemental world
3. Beholding the sun at midnight
4. Meeting with the upper and lower gods

In the imagery of the Isis mysteries this path was described by the Roman author Lucius Apuleius *(c.* AD 124–70) in *The Golden Ass* or *Metamorphoses:*

> I have arrived at the boundary of death and have stepped on
> the threshold of Proserpina [Persephone].
>   I have gone through all the elements and have come back.
>   At midnight I have seen the sun in a blinding white radiance.
>   I have approached the gods above and below face to face,
> and have worshipped them in their immediate presence.[9]

Now we can describe the connection between the four parts of the mass and the old mysteries as follows:

1. In the mysteries the aspirant was prepared for his crossing of the threshold by the teaching of old wisdom. At this stage he had to take in the message of the world on the other side. The mass has here the proclamation of the Gospel.
2. Then offerings were made to penetrate more deeply into hidden reality. Those who want to know the secrets behind visible reality have to offer themselves. In the corresponding part of the Eucharist, the offertory, the four elements appear: earth (bread), water (wine and water in the chalice), air (incense) and fire (the burning of the incense).
3. In the third phase the aspirant dwelled in the higher world. In the Egyptian mysteries that was the stage of the initiation sleep that took place for three days in a closed space or sarcophagus. One beheld the sun through the physical earth. At the altar the light of the risen Christ appears as the aura of the transubstantiated substances.
4. Finally the aspirant experienced union with the divine world. He stood eye to eye with the Godhead. Now only could he call himself an initiate. In the communion, union takes place with the being of the risen Christ. Those who take the communion become part of his body and blood.

For the Church Fathers the relation of the Eucharist with initiation was self-evident. Clement of Alexandria *(c.* 150–*c.* 212) wrote about the Eucharist in terms of initiation. He used expressions from the Dionysus mysteries. It is presumed that he himself, before he adopted Christianity, went through initiation in these mysteries. In the following passage he made clear that Christ is the fulfilment of these pre-Christian prophecies and expectations:

> Oh how truly sacred are the mysteries! Oh how pure is the
> light! By the light of torches I am surrounded in order that I
> can behold heaven and God. I become sanctified because I am
> being initiated in the mysteries. The Lord is the hierophant.
> He imprints, by the illumination, his seal on the initiate,
> and gives him who has embraced the faith into the hands of
> the Father, that he be preserved for eternity. These are the
> Bacchus feasts of my mysteries. If you wish, let yourself also be
> initiated. Together with the angels you will dance the sacred
> dance round about the ... one sole God, and the Logos of God
> will join in our songs of praise.[10]

This hymn is not about a return to the old mysteries, but about the relation of the Christian mysteries with what preceded them. For the early Christians it was self-evident that the Logos, the Creator Word, that was incarnated in Jesus, was also actively working in pre-Christian humanity. In this connection they spoke of *logos spermatikos,* the word that is present as a seed, a divine spark, in each human being, and flowered in the best representatives of pre-Christian humanity. In Clement of Alexandria this way of thinking culminated in the sentence, 'Through the Logos the whole world has become like Athens and Greece.'[11]

If we go back to the first documents that describe something of the early Eucharist, we repeatedly come across terms from the pre-Christian mysteries. The meal of bread and wine alone already was called *mysterion.* (The even older name was 'the Lord's meal'). The outer character of this meal was also that of a mystery act. Only the first part of the Eucharist service (the Gospel reading and the sermon) was open to the public. The subsequent part was announced by the call of the deacon: 'No catechumens (candidates for baptism), none of the unbelievers, none of other faiths are present.' Only after these had left the church, and the doors were closed, was the act continued, first with a summary of the divine secrets, the Creed, in which the facts of salvation were specifically named. After the Creed the actual service of bread and wine followed.

The baptism in the first centuries after Christ was also a continuation of the old mysteries. The believer was initiated into the circle of the saints. For this reason it was necessary that the baptism was prepared by a 'mystagogic catechism,' a preparatory teaching from the mysteries.[12] The bishop instructed the believers in the meaning of baptism. Thereafter, usually in the night before Easter, an impressive series of ritual acts followed of which Hippolytus gave the most extensive description. The liturgy of baptism had the following parts:

1. In the first part a prayer was said over the water, and the oil was consecrated by the bishop. The candidates took off their clothes and abjured Satan. They then professed their belief of the Father, the Son and the Holy Spirit. Thereafter the baptism took place by completely immersion in the baptismal basin.
2. Next was the anointing of the entire body. The candidates put on a white robe. The bishop laid his hands on them and sealed their crowns with oil. They were given the kiss of peace.
3. Finally the Eucharist of Baptism was celebrated. The communion did not consist of bread and wine only. From a second cup the person who was baptised received milk and honey. Finally a cup of water was given.

With this baptism the candidate went through a rebirth. An inner change *(metanoia)*, a catharsis took place.

Next he received illumination *(photismos)* by the anointing.

Finally through the Eucharist he received the body and blood of Christ. This fulfilled the call, 'Awake, you who are sleeping, arise from the dead, the Christ shall be your light!' (Eph.5:14).

It is not hard to imagine why there used to be such suspicion and lack of understanding of what was taking place behind the closed doors of the early Christian churches. One of the many allegations levelled against them by the persecutors of the early Christians was the unlikely story that they killed and devoured their own children at the altar. Another reproach was that if men and women came together, lewd acts were committed. So strict was the secrecy maintained by the first Christians that even under the greatest torture they did not reveal their secrets. Thus the Roman Governor Plinius lamented in AD 112 or 113 in a letter to Emperor Trajan:

> These accused Christians assured me that their whole guilt or error consisted in their custom to come together before sunrise on a certain day and sing hymns to Christ, as if to a god,* ... Therefore I considered it especially necessary to have two girls, who were called deaconesses, forced to tell the truth by torture. I have found nothing but sheer, erroneous superstition. Thereafter I adjourned the investigation and I turn to you for advice.[13]

It is evident from the letter that Plinius, in spite of his torture, did not find what he was looking for. Strict silence was the reason why the Eucharist, but also the other sacraments, were kept hidden in early Christianity for over two centuries. Not until later, and very gradually, did what took place behind those closed doors become known.

Clement and Origen gave indications in their writings regarding the fourfold structure of the service.[14] They described the liturgical form of the Eucharist as follows:

1. Reading from the Old and New Testaments and sermon. Then those not baptised left the church with a blessing.
2. Kiss of peace and giving of the offering gifts.
3. Prayer and thanksgiving; consecration of the substances. The Lord's Prayer.
4. The last part was introduced with the words of the celebrating priest: 'The Holy of Holies!' Communion with bread and wine at the altar.

How this fourfold form came into being from the Last Supper was not documented. At the time of Clement and Origen it was already more or less fixed. As it was experienced by the first Christians, the *content*

---

* For the word 'hymns' Plinius used the Latin word *carmen,* which means an incantation to call on the gods, a magical invocation.

of the sacrament was an unbroken continuation of the Last Supper ('Do this in remembrance of me'). The *form* of the sacrament is a continuation of the four 'mystery stages' (Rudolf Steiner's term) from pre-Christian initiation. For the first Christians that was not 'foreign' or strange, but familiar reality. We saw earlier that the terminology of the classical mysteries was also the language of early Christianity.

The sacrament in Anne Catherine Emmerich's visions

Apart from this historical description, which makes a part of the development accessible, in the works of the mystics we find countless references that give us a vivid picture of the origin and development of the sacrament. Here I want to quote part of the description dictated by the mystic Anne Catherine Emmerich (1774–1824) to Clemens Brentano. From her childhood she had visions of the life of Jesus Christ, which in the year 1812 spontaneously led to the stigmata. Since then, every year during Passion time, particularly on Good Friday, she lived through all the stages of the passion of Christ. She followed him on all his ways to Golgotha, and dictated the events which she described into the smallest details. Her *Dolorous Passion of our Lord Jesus Christ* alone takes up over 300 pages.

In her description of the Last Supper, more so than in the reports in the gospels, something is recognisable of the future sacrament of bread and wine. We must, of course, remember that Anne Catherine Emmerich was familiar with the Catholic mass and viewed things differently than the evangelists.

> Jesus' place was between Peter and John. The doors were closed, for everything was conducted with secrecy and solemnity. When the cover of the chalice had been removed and taken back to the recess in the back of the Coenaculum, Jesus prayed and uttered some very solemn words. I saw that he was explaining the Last Supper to the apostles, as also the ceremonies that were to accompany it. It reminded me of a priest teaching others the Holy Mass.
>
> ... He next blessed the Passover loaves and, I think, the oil also that was standing near, he elevated the plate with

bread with both hands, raised his eyes toward heaven, prayed, offered, set it down on the table, and again covered it. Then taking the chalice, he received into it wine and water, the former poured by Peter, the latter by John. The water he blessed before it was poured into the chalice. He then added a little more water from the small spoon, blessed the chalice, raised it on high, praying and offering, and set it down again.

... I do not know whether these ceremonies were performed in this precise order, but these and all the others that reminded me so much of the Holy Mass, I looked upon with deep emotion.

During all this time Jesus was becoming more and more collected. He said to the apostles that he was now about to give them all that he possessed, even his very self. He seemed to be pouring out his whole being in love, and I saw him becoming perfectly transparent. He looked like a luminous apparition.

In profound recollection and prayer, Jesus next broke the bread into several morsels and laid them one over another on the plate. With the tip of his finger he broke off a scrap from the first morsel and let it fall into the chalice.[15]

These descriptions are so much more detailed than those of the evangelists, and they give us a very clear picture of the 'priestly' nature of these acts. Concurrent with the Last Supper, Jesus gave his disciples a mystagogy, an initiation into the meaning of the mysteries. The disciples were drawn into the act as deacons: Peter, the passionate disciple, served the wine, and John, who had gone through catharsis, served the water. Even the ritual act of uniting bread and wine, which also occurs in the mass as well as in the Act of Consecration of Man, was performed here. In the subsequent description we can follow the invisible part of the sacramental act:

Again Jesus prayed and taught. His words, glowing with fire and light, came forth from his mouth and entered into all the apostles, excepting Judas. He took the plate with the morsels of bread (I do not remember whether he had placed it on the chalice or not) and said: 'Take and eat. This is my body which is given for you.' While saying these words, he stretched forth his right hand over it, as if giving a blessing, and as he did so, a brilliant light emanated from him. His words were luminous as was the bread which, as a body of light, entered the mouths of the apostles. It was as if Jesus himself flowed into them. I saw all of them penetrated with light, bathed in light. Judas alone was in darkness ...

He was as if passing over into what he was giving ...

When he administered his body and blood to the apostles, it appeared to me as if he emptied himself, as if he poured himself out in tender love. It is inexpressible.

... Jesus' turning to the right and left was full of gravity, as he always was when engaged in prayer. Every action indicated the institution of the Holy Mass ...

Jesus now gave to the apostles an instruction full of mystery. He told them how they were to preserve the blessed sacrament in memory of him until the end of the world.[16]

Thereupon an anointing took place of the apostles John and Peter. He told them that after receiving the Holy Spirit they would consecrate bread and wine for the first time, and would also anoint the other apostles after Pentecost. Anne Catherine Emmerich then described how after Pentecost Peter and John celebrated the sacrament and how they went out into the world and ordained additional priests by anointing the other apostles. During their absence the consecrated space of the Last Supper was guarded by Joseph of Arimathea and Nicodemus, two persons who were of great significance for the further development of Christianity.

Finally, when she looked back on the Last Supper, Anne Catherine Emmerich saw next to Christ the image of Melchizedek. Now the circle that began with the priesthood of Melchizedek is closed:

I saw Abraham kneel before an altar. I saw a holy man approach Abraham, who placed the same chalice that Jesus had in his hands in front of Abraham on the altar. I saw that this man had a sort of radiance like wings shining from his shoulders, to indicate that he was an angel. This was Melchizedek.

She described that the chalice of the Last Supper had its origin in the mysteries of El-Elyon, the Most High God who was worshipped by Melchizedek:

> When Abraham received the secret of Melchizedek, it was also revealed to him that the priest of the Most High (Melchizedek) would celebrate for Him the offering that would be instituted by the Messiah and would last forever.

In other words, with the visible picture of the Last Supper she saw the appearance of the spiritual image of the priest of the Most High God, Melchizedek, who celebrated the sacrament of bread and wine as a foreshadowing. And again we see the expression, 'It reminded me of the Holy Mass.'

> Melchizedek also blessed Abraham. I saw that this was a foreshadowing, as if he ordained him as priest, for Abraham already received the promise that from him the flesh and blood of the Messiah would appear.

This description shows that the Last Supper, although it brought a renewal of the ritual act, is at the same time a continuation of what began with Melchizedek. Rudolf Frieling, one of the founders of the Christian Community, spoke of 'the metamorphosis of the Eucharist.'[17] The concept of metamorphosis is used for changes in appearance of living beings, such as plants. In a certain sense the seed of the Eucharist was sown already when Melchizedek brought the bread and wine. For centuries this seed remained hidden, until it burst open with the Last Supper. Thereafter the sacrament grew in the days after the Resurrection, when Christ himself celebrated the meal with his disciples. The Eucharist came into its own at Pentecost. Then it could be continued outside the circle of disciples. With this, however, the metamorphosis did not by any means come to an end. In the following chapters we will see how the meal of bread and wine developed further.

Even this summary of the development of the Eucharist in the first three centuries shows that the meal of bread and wine runs like a golden thread through Christianity from the very beginning.

Only later, from the year 393, when the canon of the four gospels was formed, did Christianity begin to develop into doctrine and dogma. But the strongest and deepest connection with the living Christ is formed even today by the meal in which he gives himself to us.

7

The Development of the Eucharist

The twelve apostles

The Christian sacrament began with the one Last Supper and developed into a multiplicity of ritual forms. But all those different forms are offshoots from the same source. The development of the Eucharist is like the course of a river: a stream wells up out of one spring, and gradually it grows in size and fans out into a delta with multiple streams. This movement has been present in Christianity from the beginning. Christ himself brought about a Christendom would not be a matter of one sole omniscient, authoritative church (despite the fact that even today some churches make that claim).

The process began already with the calling of the apostles. The Gospel of Mark (3:14,16) twice uses the unusual words for this: 'Christ created the twelve' *(epoiēsen tous dōdeka)*. The circle of twelve was not arbitrarily put together, but it manifests a creative process. We can follow precisely how tensions, frictions, jealousy and struggles about their ranking arose among the quite outspoken characters of the twelve disciples. In all too human words, Christ could have made things easier for himself if he had not chosen such outspoken personalities. Apparently he did not want 'twelve meek sheep' who would say 'Yes sir' to all he said, but individuals with their own will and their own views.

Another human comparison shows the contrast with more common forms of leadership. When a spiritual leader reaches the end of their activities they will usually appoint a successor, someone who has to continue their life work and mission. We are also familiar with this phenomenon in political and economic life. Of course, the Roman Catholic Church is based on the primacy of Simon Peter, 'On this rock I will build my congregation' (Matt.16:18), but the gospels show time and again that this does not mean that Simon Peter is the best of all. Christ gave each disciple a task of his own that corresponded with his potential. Thus Christ had to show Peter his own way beside that of John when he said to him after the resurrection, 'If I choose for him to remain until my coming, it does not concern you: Follow me!' (John 21:22).

Christianity is not a matter of obedience, but of unity in diversity. The word 'obedience' never even appears in any of Jesus' statements. Many times he spoke about hearing as a sense with which human beings can develop spiritual qualities, but he never demanded obedience of his followers.

This is powerfully expressed at Pentecost. Christianity came to manifestation in twelvefold ways. Each of the apostles spoke his own language – but in such a way that each could understand the other. In a certain sense the future image of Christianity came to manifestation for the first time at Pentecost. One of my colleagues once expressed this elusive character of Pentecost, which is not a status quo, but a lightning strike from a clear sky, with the words, 'Pentecost occurred – thereafter it withdrew again into the future.' But we can witness that out of the first Pentecost a whole palette of variations on one theme came into being.

Tradition tells us that at Pentecost each of the twelve apostles professed Christianity in his own way. The Apostles' Creed, one of the oldest forms of the Creed, is built up of twelve sentences that in early Christianity were already viewed as pronouncements of the twelve apostles.[1]

Tradition also reports that after Pentecost Christianity spread in all directions. If we try to form a picture of all those movements, we become conscious of the gigantic area the disciples covered:

- Peter went to Rome. There he was always venerated as the precursor of the Roman Catholic popes.
- John, the brother of James (one of the two sons of Zebedee), worked in the seven congregations in Asia Minor.
- His brother, James the Just, travelled to Spain. Tradition says that he was buried in Santiago de Compostela.
- Andrew worked in the Roman province of Achaia, Greece, with its capital of Corinth. The Russians consider Andrew as

their apostle, because he also worked in Scythia, the area
north of the Black Sea.
- Philip went to Phrygia and Galatia in Asia Minor.
- Thomas worked in India, where even today the St Thomas
  Christians have their own church.
- Bartholomew went to Cilicia in Asia Minor.
- Matthew left tracks down into Ethiopia. There also an
  individual form of Christianity came into being.
- Mark is viewed as the first bishop of the Coptic Church
  in Egypt.
- Simon the Zealot went to Persia (Iran).
- Judas Thaddeus went to Mesopotamia (Iraq).
- And Matthias, who filled the vacancy left by Judas Iscariot,
  worked in Palestine.

There is a document dating back to the year 100 called the *didache*,
the teaching of the twelve apostles, that contains the oldest preserved
texts of the Eucharist. Undoubtedly, so soon after the foundation of
Christianity, original texts written by apostles found their way into
this document.

The apostles transferred their power and working to their successors
by the laying on of hands. Thus arose the 'apostolic succession' – the
successor becomes part of a stream that connects him with the first
apostles, and through them with Christ. This principle is practised
even today in the Roman Catholic Church, where the Pope fills the
position of Peter and maintains the apostolic succession.

Before we follow the Eucharist in its further development we have
take a step back in time to follow another track. In the previous
chapter it was said that the Eucharist was celebrated already before
Pentecost in the circle of apostles by James the Nazirite. He was also
called 'the brother of the Lord'. Although he did not belong to the
twelve, he held an important place in Jerusalem in the earliest days of
Christianity. His name as brother of Jesus was mentioned in passing
by Mark (6:3). Paul came to know James (Gal.1:19) as the head of the
congregation in Jerusalem, when the latter played a leading role in the
council of the Apostles described in Acts 15:6–29.

There are many texts from early Christianity in which the role of James the Nazirite is described. For instance, the chronicler Hegesippus (died *c.* 180) wrote about him, 'He was holy from his birth. Neither wine nor liquor did he enjoy. He also did not shave his hair.'[2] These were rules of the Nazirites, an ascetic movement with which John the Baptist also had connections. Hegesippus' description is of a strict ascetic, who had made the temple his home: 'Thus he always went alone to the temple. There he was seen continually kneeling and beseeching God to redeem his people. He did that so incessantly that his knees were swollen like those of a camel.' The fact that James could enter the temple without being accompanied means that he had exceptional privileges there.

Early traditions also tell that although James was a step-brother of Jesus, there was a remarkable resemblance in his face and bearing. From far and near the first Christians came to see James, because they could then make a picture of Jesus for themselves. The resemblance was not only an outer one. In the time between Ascension and Pentecost of the year 33 the fervent prayer of James for insight was answered. According to St Jerome the answer came from the Resurrected One himself in the form of the Eucharist. Subsequently James, as the first follower of the Resurrected One, celebrated the meal for the other disciples, and thus became the first presbyter (elder) of Christendom. At the same time he became the first bishop of the Jewish-Christian congregation in Jerusalem. This community held strictly to Jewish tradition. This was diametrically opposed to the views of Paul, the apostle to the Gentiles, who did not require adherence to Jewish laws for non-Jews. The very fact that there were these two different forms of early Christianity shows the need for more than one form.

Without James, Christianity in Jerusalem was inconceivable. According to the above tradition he also formed the bridge between the Risen Christ and the twelve disciples, by laying his hands on them (and on others). On the other hand, Paul also formed the important bridge between the Christianity of the Jews and that of the Gentiles. Each of the disciples held a one-sided, but indispensable place in the spread of Christianity. The ubiquity of the Risen One became visible in their work. Later, part of the work of the twelve apostles was transferred by the laying on of hands to the first seven deacons, who tended the sacramental life in the congregation (Acts 6:3–7).

But we know that this ritual act was not at all new in Christianity. It existed in countless pre-Christian rituals. A striking expression of this act was painted by Rembrandt (1606–69) in *The Blessing of Jacob.* Like no other, Rembrandt was able to depict the spiritual power of this act, as this painting shows. Jacob, now blind, blessed his grandson Ephraim. In doing this he broke with the Jewish tradition that the grandfather had to bless his eldest grandson. Joseph, his son, still tried to intervene in order to let the eldest grandson receive the blessing, but old Jacob had his own reasons to lay his hand on the youngest child, Ephraim.

Rembrandt was a master in *noctiluca,* light of the night, that springs forth out of the darkness without demonstrable source. Light, spiritual light, shines from the hand of the grandfather, surrounds the face of the grandchild, and shines to the heart of the child. Ephraim receives this light with a gesture of deep devotion. The blessing he receives will accompany him for the rest of his life. For that was

Figure 15. Rembrandt, The Blessing of Jacob, *(1656, Gemäldegalerie alter Meister, Kassel).*

the intention of the laying on of hands in the Old Testament: a blessing once given could not be taken back. The blessing lived on in the one who had received it for the rest of his life. In Christianity this ritual act was continued without interruption. Every stream in Christianity thus formed its own continuity in the apostolic succession.

In the early years of Christianity the Eucharist was never just a celebration in remembrance of the Last Supper. In the altar service Christ is 'cited' in two meanings of the word. Not only is there a literal citation of Christ's words during the Last Supper when he gave the bread and wine to the disciples; in addition, the concept of 'citing' can also be used to evoke someone's presence, as in 'inciting'. In this sense the early Christians experienced that the Risen One himself fulfilled their word and ritual act. Ignatius of Antioch (c. 35 – c. 107) spoke about the Eucharist as the elixir of immortality: 'Breaking bread, which is the elixir of immortality, the antidote to death, in order that we shall always live in Christ.'[3] We find the word eucharist (from Greek *eucharistos,* thankful) in the words Christ spoke over the bread and wine during the Last Supper.

The first Christians experienced the meal of bread and wine as 'armour' in the daily battle of life. Cyprian (c. 200–258), bishop of Carthage, described in his 57th letter the custom to receive the meal of Christ as necessary preparation for a martyr's death:

> That we may not leave those whom we stir up and exhort to
> the battle unarmed and naked, but may fortify them with the
> protection of Christ's body and blood ... First of all, he cannot
> be fitted for martyrdom who is not armed for the contest by
> the Church; and his spirit is deficient which the Eucharist
> received does not raise and stimulate.[4]

Parting of the ways

It was not until late in the development of the Eucharist that doubts began to rise as to the 'ubiquity' of Christ in the sacrament. Taking a bird's eye view over this development, a number of clear steps can be discerned. The canon of the mass (a prayer during the transubstantiation) was given its more or less definitive form by Pope Gregory the Great (590–604). For him the concept of the mass as an offering plays a greater role than before: 'In this mystery of the Holy Mass Christ is sacrificed anew for us.'

However, this also brought an impure element into the Eucharist, for from the seventh century on, masses were ordered for personal purposes against payment. In the course of this development, in the eighth and ninth centuries a Requiem Mass came into being that was celebrated by the priest without a congregation present. Apart from the questionable forms of masses as commodities, concurrent with this we witness the development of speaking in the first person singular. It is part of the process of individualisation that began in Europe. The Eastern (Orthodox) Church did not follow in this development. In the eleventh century there is a parting of the ways between the Western and Eastern Churches.

In the Eastern Church the separation between the sacred and the faithful is made visible in the iconostasis. Behind this screen of icons the mass is enacted, mostly unseen by, and sometimes also inaudible (whispered) to the congregation. In the Greek Orthodox mass before the Creed is read the priest calls, 'The doors, the doors!' in direct continuation of the mass in early Christianity, when the doors were closed to those who had not been baptised.

Only during the reading of the gospel (when the gospel is carried in procession around the church), in a second procession with the substances of the meal, and during the offertory, are the doors of the iconostasis opened, and the holy of holies becomes visible. Just as in the old mysteries, the priest is the mystagogue who works in secret. In essence divine liturgy (as the Eucharist is called in the Orthodox church) is a divine act, with which the celebrant and the congregation concur and in which they participate.

The Eastern Church and also St Thomas Christians in India, make a connection between the development of the sacraments and the fifty days between Golgotha and Pentecost. During that time the Risen One established the seven sacraments and taught them to the disciples. The Eastern Church consistently speaks of the Resurrection Meal rather than the Last Supper. Also, the prayer invoking the Holy Spirit *(epiclesis)* is of central importance, as is the presence *(parousia)* of the Risen One.

Rudolf Frieling sometimes compared this ritual form with the old German custom of letting the children only come into the room when the candles on the Christmas tree had been lighted. Behind closed doors, hidden to the eye, everything was made ready – then the doors were opened and the miracle was revealed.

The purpose in the Western Church is to enable the congregation to participate in all the acts from beginning to end. From the priest's entering to leaving the church, the congregation is literally and figuratively present – albeit that for a long time several prayers were still whispered by the priest.

One of the most noteworthy differences between the Western and Eastern Churches is the way they regard the death on the cross and the resurrection. These differences led not only to differences in theology and dogma, but also to different forms in the service. In the Middle Ages in western Europe the view was that the sacraments originated in the passion of Christ. (In Chapter 6 we saw the seven sacraments springing from the wounds of the Crucified One. Thomas Aquinas represented a similar view, that the sacraments arose *ex virtute passionis,* from the virtue of Christ's passion.)

From the Middle Ages, the emphasis of the Western Church was on the death on the cross, and to a lesser extent on the resurrection and ascension. Finally, Protestantism connected the sacrament of bread and wine exclusively with the Last Supper, and commemorated 'the death of the Lord.'

From the twelfth to the fourteenth century new prayers developed in the mass; the offertory received a distinct character, at first especially in Spain, France and Ireland and from there spreading in the Roman Catholic mass. In this period also the custom developed of restricting the communion to the bread, denying wine from the chalice. This custom became the established rule at the Council of Constance in 1415. This was based on the idea that outside the Church no salvation is to be found, and that the Church itself, as the representative of Christ, guarantees the salvation of the faithful. The chalice was always viewed as connected with the salvation of the human being ('the cup of salvation'), whereas the bread was connected with 'redemption of sin, transgressions and negligence.' Thus bread and wine were connected with the past and future of human beings. By denying them the chalice the Church created an obstacle for human beings to have an autonomous relationship with their own future.

From the fourteenth to the sixteenth century growing resistance arose against the abuses in the Church, in particular against the mass as something that could be bought and sold, as well as against the trade in indulgences. In this dark period, in which efforts were made to reform the Church, there were also growing doubts as to the reality of the transubstantiation. Sown by the philosophical battle between the realists and nominalists, this doubt existed already in the time of Scholasticism in the Middle Ages. The realists represented the view that words express a reality (conceptual realism), but for the nominalists, words were nothing but concepts and symbols without any reality that just represent arbitrary meanings created by human thinking.

In this philosophical dispute, nominalism was victorious, not only as a philosophical stream, but also in the practice of science, and even increasingly in our view of life: thoughts and feelings were less and less experienced as a reality. In our day we are told again and again that they have no relation to objective reality, which leads its own life without our realising it.

Thus, in the Reformation, the reality of the sacraments is relativised – they are reduced to mere symbols. A striking illustration of this conflict between nominalist and realist thinking is the discussion between the two Reformers Luther (1483–1546) and Zwingli (1484–1531). Zwingli did not view the words spoken over the bread and wine as a spiritual reality. 'This *is* my body,' should not be taken literally. Actually Christ meant to say, 'This *signifies* my body.' Although Luther was not able to counter this view philosophically, he held fast to the actual reality of the transubstantiation: 'This *is* my body.'

In England, John Wycliff (1320–1384) rejected the old doctrine of the transubstantiation. He said that bread and wine were mere symbols of the presence of Christ. 'It is an error,' wrote Wycliff, 'that by the transubstantiation in the mass the priest creates the body of Christ.' The mass was condemned even more radically in the Protestant Heidelberg Catechism: 'The mass is nothing other than a repudiation of the sole true offering and the suffering of Christ. It is a cursed idolatry.'

We have to realise that such sharp words were reactions to the countless abuses in the Roman Catholic Church at the time, which also came to expression in the mass. Luther even spoke of 'this dragon tail, the mass, that has begot much vermin and scum of all kinds of idolatry.'

In response to these abuses, five of the seven sacraments were abolished in the Reformation. Only the baptism and the Eucharist, in greatly reduced form, remained. In the Protestant liturgy the offertory (part 2) and the transubstantiation (part 3) have disappeared. Only the scripture reading, hymns, prayers and sermon are still left, and now and then the communion is added to this liturgy (which was in effect the first part of the old mass).

Even in the twentieth century the sacrament in Calvinist churches was celebrated at tables. In this way Calvin expressed 'that by his death and resurrection Christ gave humanity rest.' In Calvinism there is the view that not only by the fall, but also by being an accessory to the crucifixion, humanity is far removed from God. Through faith, human beings may again be made righteous by God (the doctrine of justification). Therefore, according to Protestantism, there is no reason to repeat the sacrifice of Christ in an 'unbloody continuation' (to use the words of the Catholic Church). Here a theological dispute comes to light about the question whether the sacrifice of Christ was made 'once for all time' (Protestantism), or whether an inner renewal remains necessary for human beings. The view of Catholicism is that human beings can themselves collaborate in the creation by inwardly purifying themselves and receiving the grace of Christ in the form of bread and wine.

Both have their own interpretations of these points of view, but both also cover the entire spectrum from complete resignation to hyper-tension. Contradictory as it sounds, both also recognise the sinfulness of humanity. Protestantism does this explicitly with the words 'original sin': humanity rejected the sacrifice of Christ on the cross, and for this reason we never know for sure whether what we do is good. Catholicism did it implicitly by pointing to 'our sins, transgressions and negligence' which can be taken away only by the mediation of the Church (absolution). To this 'grace upon grace' through the sacraments can be added. What we put into the world out of ourselves is inferior to that. Life outside the Church is therefore inconceivable for the 'salvation of the soul'.

In conclusion we can add a few more words on recent developments. The Catholic mass was thoroughly revised by the Second Vatican Council (1962–65). The best known changes are the use of the vernacular instead of Latin, and the priest facing the congregation. More recently, in 2007, under the influence of Pope Benedict XVI, the Latin mass was also allowed again.

The Act of Consecration of Man, to which a separate chapter is devoted, shows the Eucharist in its original four parts. The basic form of the Christian ritual is recognisable. The direction which celebrant faces is 'traditional'. A comparison with the early forms of the mass shows that this is not a 'restoration effort', but that in the Act of Consecration of Man the original idea is manifest in a new way.

8

Christianity and Renewal

To form a concrete picture of what religious renewal means we have to consider the question of what is new? Christ himself used this word several times to indicate that he brought something that was not there before. The Greek language has two words for 'new': *neos* and *kainos*. The word *neos* expresses something that is new in the sense of an addition in arithmetic, something quantitative, the next one in a series. The word *kainos* is used for something that is completely new, different from what was before. It is a qualitative concept. For instance, Christ used *kainos* in the sentence, 'A new task and aim I give you' (John 13:34). Luke used the same word in, 'This cup is the new covenant *(kainē diathēkē)* with God, established through my blood which is shed for you,' spoken by Christ during the Last Supper (Luke 22:20).

In early Christianity the awareness of a new commandment, a new covenant, the beginning of a new creation, was vividly present. In the midst of an old, mostly decadent world, Christianity was a movement that was extremely alive. The persecution of Christians in ancient Rome did not result in decimating or eradicating them, but actually in fostering a sense of self-worth. Eusebius wrote this quite frankly in his *Church History* when he quoted Tertullian:

> Read your history books. There you will find that Nero was the first to persecute our church; that after he had prevented its growth in Rome, he ranted and raved against all Christians. We are proud that such a person was the first to act against us. For all who know Nero have to know that whatever was particularly good was denounced by him.[1]

A notably new element that distinguished the Christians from their predecessors was the strength of the community. This was true primarily for the celebration of the sacraments. Unlike in the pre-Christian mysteries, where a person was individually prepared for his initiation, the sacraments take place in community. We see this element also in the daily life of the early Christians. 'And all who found the faith practised community in all things. They sold their belongings and shared the proceeds among each other, according to the needs of each individual.' (Acts 2:44f).

But this form of 'Christian communism' did not develop out of a class struggle or dictatorship, but 'from above', out of the sacramental community.

Rudolf Steiner went even further to show what the essentially new aspect of Christianity was:

> The Christian Mystery was to replace the many Mysteries of
> the ancient world with its unique, archetypal Mystery-event.
> In Jesus the *Logos* had become flesh, and he was to become the
> teacher of initiation to all humanity. His community of mystai
> was to be the human race. In place of the old principle of
> selecting individuals, there was to be the gathering together of
> all. Hence everyone was enabled to become *mystes,* insofar they
> were sufficiently mature to do so. The Gospel is proclaimed
> to all, and whoever has an ear to hear is eager to fathom its
> mysteries; the heart of each has the decisive voice.
>
> Thus it was no longer a case of introducing one person or
> another into the temples of the Mysteries, but of the word
> spoken to all and heard now with more, now with less clarity
> and strength. And it will be left to the *daimon,* the angel in
> a person's own breast, to decide how far one's initiation can
> proceed. The Mystery-temple is the entire world.
>
> ... There is no secrecy; the way opens out for all.[2]

It would be hard to make a more radical statement about the renewal that Christianity brought. Here we witness an essential difference between the pre-Christian and Christian mysteries: the mysteries came out in the open.

In addition to this community element Christ brought another radical renewal. We find this, among other places, in the letter to the congregation in Pergamum in the Apocalypse where the Risen One announced:

> To him who overcomes I will give of the hidden manna and a
> white stone on which a new [*kainos*] name is written which no
> one knows except he who receives it (Rev.2:17).

In antiquity such stones were used for voting in cases of deciding
the fate of someone or something. In the future creation – to
which this passage refers – human beings will have received the
'right to vote' they will have become mature, emancipated, and can
become co-creators with the divine world. This is only possible by
developing the I, not the egoistic, all-too-human I, but the higher
self that is here symbolised in the shining white stone. We can
already recognise a little of this unique quality in daily life, when
someone puts their own stamp on their work and gives it a quality
of its own. C.G. Jung spoke in this context of 'individuation'. The
I gives us the potential of bringing something new into the world,
something unique.

We find an expansion and sequel to the symbolism of the white
stone in the letter to the Philadelphians, in which Christ said:

> Him who overcomes I will make a pillar in the temple of my
> divine Father ... And I will inscribe on him ... my own name,
> which is new [*kainos*] (Rev.3:12).

The human I has become a 'pillar of support' in God's temple.
Together these separate pillars carry the roof: every I becomes part of
the community 'which knows Christ in freedom as its helping guide,'
as it is expressed in the Act of Consecration of Man.

Thus we have summarised a few essential characteristics of
Christianity, as intended by Christ himself, in three key words: I –
Community – Freedom.

From the perspective of these three words we return to the
sacrament of bread and wine – with the question of renewal of the
Christian ritual.

In the previous chapter it was briefly mentioned that in the
eighth and ninth centuries we could witness the first indications of
individualisation. In Spain, France and Ireland (where in the ninth
century the Grail stories arose) personal devotion developed in the
mass. The liturgical texts and prayers were spoken in the first person

singular. In the old mass it was a liturgical rule that the celebrant spoke 'to the Father through Christ.' Now however, arose a form in which the I spoke directly to 'Thee', to Christ. The mass underwent a development from 'we' to 'I'.

As we so often see in new developments, the pendulum soon swung too far: before long there was a market in masses-for-sale. It is the familiar inevitable shadow as the side-effect of light. When the I announces itself, the lower ego also comes to the fore.

In brief, renewal of the ritual begins with the growing consciousness of the I. But in isolation, separate from the community, the I has no meaning, just as one sole pillar that supports nothing has no purpose. Similarly, renewal of the Christian ritual is indissolubly linked with development of the I-in-community. Once you have become 'yourself', the next step is to make this 'yourself' available to the community in freedom. The Greek expression for this is *diakonia*. Rudolf Steiner once explained this principle in the following passage. His formulation enables us to recognise where true renewal takes place in concrete communities.

When people let their feelings shine together of their own free will this creates something which again goes beyond the purely emancipated human being. The emancipated human being has an individual soul; this will never be lost once it has been gained. But when people come together voluntarily they group around focal points and this gives opportunities to spirits to act like a kind of group soul but in a very different way from the group souls of old. All the earlier group souls were spirits that made human beings unfree. These new spirits, however, are compatible with complete freedom, maintaining the individual nature of people. We may actually say that they manage to survive, in some respect, thanks to human unity; it will be due to human souls themselves to offer the opportunity to as many of those higher souls as possible to descend into the human realm. The more associations are formed, and the more community feeling develops in complete freedom, the more sublime spirits will come down to humanity and the faster will planet Earth be made spiritual.

We see, therefore, that to get an idea at all of future evolution people must thoroughly understand the character of group soul nature. Otherwise it may happen that emancipated on its own on Earth the individual human soul will fail to make connection and then turn into a kind of elemental spirit itself. And elementals developed from human beings would be of a truly evil kind.

Renewal in the Act of Consecration of Man

We can now approach this aspect more concretely with the aid of texts from the Act of Consecration of Man. In 1922 the Christian Community, Movement for Religious Renewal, came into being with the help of Rudolf Steiner. In this renewal movement the Act of Consecration of Man occupies a central position. The sacrament of bread and wine is presented and celebrated in a new form. The Christian Community does not act as the only true church, but as a part of Christendom as a whole. This awareness sounds in the broadest sense of the word in the following sentence from the Creed of the Christian Community: 'Communities whose members feel the Christ within themselves may feel united in a church to which all belong who are aware of the health-bringing power of the Christ.' This is not the place to expound on the aims of the Christian Community and how the movement came into being.

It would be naive to think that the intended religious renewal is already completely realised in the Christian Community. A person who knew the Christian Community once said, 'The difference is in the content; the people are just like everywhere else.' Therefore, this newness, which is connected with complete freedom and respect for the other, can only be achieved by trial and error. Taking freedom for yourself makes life easier; giving freedom to another usually makes life more complicated. This freedom not only implies that there are no dogmas or official doctrines in the Christian Community, but also that children – and even adults – do not need to confess their faith. Membership is a matter of making a well-considered, adult decision. A person who is baptised or a young person who is confirmed is not 'inducted' as a member of the church. The ordained priest is free in his teaching. The only binding aspect in the Christian Community are the seven sacraments; they are celebrated along fixed forms.

As part of this new form of community, which is connected with free will, the sacrament of bread and wine also received a new name, the Act of Consecration of Man. This indicates something of the intention of this community. The old mass received its name from the final words of the priest, *'Ite, missa est'*, 'Go, there is dismissal.' You can't call this a name; it is a quotation from the liturgical text. The Act of Consecration of Man begins and ends with the new name. The opening words are, 'Let us worthily fulfil the Act of Consecration of Man,' and the closing words are, 'The Act of Consecration of Man, thus it has been.' The name implies that as human beings we are not 'finished products'; a consecration is needed to become true human beings.

In antiquity it was known that it did not take much for human beings to fall back into the animal stage: *Homo homini lupus* meaning 'one human being is a wolf for another'. But can we also turn it around and say: *homo homini angelus,* 'one human being is an angel for another'? We find this idea in the writings of Dionysius the Areopagite, namely that human beings have the mission to spiritualise themselves. 'Deification' is our actual mission. We also find this task in the Hasidic Jewish tradition, where it is presented in a playful manner in the following words that have been handed down by tradition from Israel Ben Eliezer, the Baal Shem Tov:

> The Lord said: 'Let us make man after our image and likeness.'
> To whom was God speaking when he said this? He spoke to
> the human being himself. 'Come, you and I together, let us
> create the human being, because without your help I will never
> be able to make you into a real human being.'

In a certain sense, these words also express what is taking place in the Act of Consecration of Man. Our imperfect being-human is consecrated at the altar – and the Act of Consecration leaves no room for misunderstanding as to who is consecrating us. Because of this, a service which, viewed superficially, places the human being in the centre, becomes a religious service.

This does not quite suffice to indicate what is actually new in the

Act of Consecration of Man. Renewal of religious life is inconceivable without the fact of the Second Coming of Christ. Because Christ reveals himself to people in a different way than before, people who experience his presence are able to speak about him in a different way than before. In the twentieth and twenty-first centuries many people have witnessed his Second Coming.[4]

Albert Steffen (1884–1963), one of the few 'outsiders' who witnessed the celebration of the first Act of Consecration of Man in the Goetheanum in Dornach on 16 September 1922, wrote in his diary what took place in this service. Apart from an effort to render in words an overwhelming experience of spiritual reality, this fragment of Steffen's diary is also an effort to 'place' the Act of Consecration of Man in the sense of this chapter: what is new in it? What is the place of the Christian Community among other denominations?

Sunday, 16 September 1922, noon.

Today the first Act of Consecration of Man was completed on earth out of the spirit, and at which the Risen Christ was present. Rittelmeyer ordained twelve people as priests. At the conclusion, Steiner said the following words: 'You have asked me to give you out of the spirit the possibility to speak to the divine spiritual world in a rightful way, to proclaim the word of Christ. I had to muster the courage to give you an answer and to bring a ritual in the sense of Christ, to show a priestly ordination that takes in Christ.

'The Catholic Church has this ordination by apostolic succession because every priest receives his ordination from an ordained priest. This can be traced back to Christ who was the first to bestow an ordination. The Protestant Church has given up the ritual and has fallen apart. It could no longer give that which is connected with ordination ... And thus arose for me, in response to your question, the task to muster the courage to bring a new service of consecration of man born out of the spirit. This has created a connection that is not historical, but alive.'

Steffen continued in his own words:

I can say that Christ was there, for when the words of bread and wine were spoken, I saw his resurrected light-life body. It is the first time I have seen the being of Christ. His arms were outstretched and there was a radiance about his head. And I experienced then that he healed and hallowed. He was there, and is there. This certainty makes me into his proclaimer.[5]

Reduced to the shortest possible formulation, we are quite justified to call the Christian Community 'the Community of the Second Coming'. The apostolic succession, by which of old the connection was made with historic Christianity, has been broken. In its place a new succession has come into being that goes back to the first Act of Consecration of Man.

It is abundantly clear that this sacrament – and this also holds true for the other sacraments – could not have been created without the help and intercession of Rudolf Steiner. Something of the riddle of this intercession shows in a remarkable dream Friedrich Rittelmeyer had, and which he was able to verify with Rudolf Steiner. Evidently the question of the origin of the Act of Consecration of Man had also been on his mind at the time, for in one of his lucid dreams he put this question to Steiner. The latter gave him a remarkable answer in the dream: 'I had to go to a place where the German language is taught mantrically.' When shortly thereafter Rittelmeyer asked Steiner whether this dream represented reality, Steiner replied, 'Yes, only don't think of that place as if you could send a parcel there in the mail.' We might wonder – and the answer to this question is not easy to find – where that place is and how a human being can ever go there.

The formulation of a new succession could lead to the misunderstanding that only the first Act of Consecration of Man was completely real in the sense of the Second Coming, and that all later services were mere memories or shadows of it. In the Act of Consecration the presence of the living Christ is evoked. In a conversation with Rittelmeyer, Steiner expressed this in a straightforward way, 'The presence of Christ can be evoked, and will be evoked.' Rittelmeyer wondered at these words and said, 'But that is incredible.' Steiner: 'It is self-evident.'[6]

What for us human beings is unimaginable is self-evident for Christ. Where at the altar, out of a mood of reverence and devotion, the prayers of Christians rise to the living Christ, he can be present in their midst. It cannot be anything other, for the meaning of the original concept of Second Coming in the New Testament is *parousia*. This concept has four meanings: presence, arrival, aid, indwelling. All four meanings express presence of the spirit, not a distant past or an indeterminate future, but in the present.

9

The Sacrament of Bread and Wine

Unity in diversity

In the preceding chapters we have seen that in the course of the evolution of consciousness of humanity there has been a continual development of new ritual forms, which are expressions of changes in consciousness. We can recognise this in the transition from pre-Christian to Christian forms of ritual, but also in the way in which the sacrament of bread and wine has developed over the past two thousand years. In the development of an organism value judgments are not meaningful; a child is not worth less than an adult, a flower or fruit is not better than a bud or a seed. In the context of development we have used the word 'metamorphosis', a word that has its origin in the Hellenistic mystery tradition and later became part of the ordinary use of language.

In all the different forms of ritual in Christianity we always – despite their diversity – recognise the One who comes to manifestation in them. For this reason we will show several experiences in this chapter that demonstrate this essential unity.

In the gospel Christ indicated how we can come to know him after his resurrection. Thomas, the doubter, could only believe if he could see his Lord and touch him: 'Unless I see in his hands the mark of the nails and place my finger in the place where the nails were, and place my hand in his side, I cannot believe it' (John 20:25). This has become a well-known saying that is typical for our time, 'Seeing is believing'. When Thomas had overcome his doubts by doing what he wanted to do, Christ said, 'Blessed are those who have not seen and yet believe' (John 20:29 RSV).

Since ancient times these have been the two ways to spiritual reality in all forms of ritual: the way of the senses (seeing, hearing, touching, etc.) and the way of faith.

Martin Luther also called faith an organ of perception and said, 'Faith is a sixth sense that far exceeds all other senses.' For the concept of faith we could also use the term 'heart's power of vision', which sounds in the Ascension epistle of the Act of Consecration of Man. But ritual is an act in which the senses play a decisive role, for in our seeing, hearing and sense of touch the content can reveal itself. (I will come back to this later in more detail.) In the following descriptions we can easily recognise the two ways of faith and perception.

Of Thomas Aquinas we know that he had an overwhelming experience at the altar that changed him, as if by magic. In the last phase of his life while he was writing his book, *Summa Theologica,* he broke off his work from one day to the next. While he was celebrating the mass, he was overcome by a spiritual experience due to which he could no longer speak. Afterwards his secretary, Reginald of Piperno, asked him what happened to him, and Thomas answered, 'All I have written seems like straw to me after what I have seen and was revealed to me.' It is impossible to describe in words the reality of Christ at the altar. Thomas never finished his life work, fell into silence and died in 1274. Here the secret that was revealed to one person remained hidden.

Some priests are able to relate similar experiences in words. An impressive example of this is the Russian starets John of Kronstadt (1829–1909). For 53 years he celebrated the orthodox mass every day. When he celebrated early in the morning there were usually some five thousand people gathered in the cathedral to hear the 'Kronstadt Father'. He thus performed the duties of his office for hours each day into his old age, praying and celebrating, while also seeing countless visitors and receiving hundreds of letters every day. In 1964 he was canonised. His books frequently describe the sacrament of bread and wine, as well as his own experiences at the altar:

The celebration of the liturgy is a tremendous assignment,
a great ethical task for the priest. It demands the most careful,
uninterrupted preparation. The priest needs an angelic ability
to overcome passions and desires, a burning love for God and
fellow human beings. His whole being, his heart, mind and
will, have to be focused on the spirit. The will of the priest
has to correspond in full with God's will. The priest is a high
intermediary. To him has the mystery of the renewal of the

human being been entrusted. He leads the fire of the spirit to the altar and the holy gifts. For many centuries the world has waited for this awesome mystery, the manifestation of God in the body. The divine liturgy is a supra-earthly service of consecration, because God himself is inexpressibly close to the human being. Nothing on earth is so holy, exalted and life-bestowing as the sacrament.[1]

Always, when celebrating the altar service, John of Kronstadt recognised the Christ:

In the transubstantiation in the sacraments the priest must be totally convinced that what he thinks and speaks takes place immediately. He has to be completely certain of receiving the body and blood of Christ in the sacraments. As sure as I am of the fact that I breathe, with the same certainty I take my Lord Jesus Christ into myself, him who is my life, my breath, my spiritual nourishment and redemption. Who can grasp the greatness of the gift that Christ offers us in the sacrament of communion? No one, not even the intelligence of the angels! ... I am extinguished, I die in spirit when I do not celebrate for several days. I catch fire, I revive in heart and soul as soon as I celebrate and turn to prayer – not the formal, but the spiritual, sincere, fervent prayer.

The great saints such as Thomas Aquinas and John of Kronstadt are not the only ones where we find indications of the spiritual power that makes the sacrament actual, tangible reality. The priest who in all simplicity and modesty performs the daily service, as well as the faithful who full of reverence and devotion participate in the act, can also testify to it.

When I visited churches behind the Iron Curtain in the 1980s I had frequent conversations with priests of the Russian Orthodox, Armenian and Georgian churches, during which I often asked them about their experiences with the sacraments. One of them told me that one day he and his server were the only ones in his congregation. He celebrated in an empty church. He could not suppress a feeling of disappointment. During the following he had a dream. Again he saw himself at the altar.

When he turned around to the congregation, the church was filled with a multitude of angels who celebrated the mass with him.

A member of the Christian Community attended a mass in Rome once. Quite unexpectedly, when the priest lifted up the consecrated bread, he saw the aura of the Risen Christ as a golden splendour around the host. Here spiritual perception was closely connected with the visible act at the altar. This is a well-known occurrence which for clairvoyant perception recurs in many different guises. If a religious liturgy is worthily celebrated, spiritual gold can become manifest at the altar. I will relate one more of the many, often spontaneous experiences with this 'quintessence' which I have been privileged to hear from members of our congregation.

Before the Second World War, a seventeen-year-old girl found a book by Friedrich Rittelmeyer with a description of the Act of Consecration of Man. Reading this book made her curious to see it in action. When she was eighteen she found the address of a Christian Community. In order to attend the service she had to travel the previous day and stay overnight in a different town. The Act of Consecration of Man that she attended the next morning for the first time was too much for her. Disillusioned she left the church, certain that this was the first and the last service of the Christian Community she would attend. But things worked out differently.

War broke out. In the dramatic time that followed, this young woman lived with a prayer that kept coming back to her: 'Let me meet the people in my life who can tell me about Christ.' After the war she worked as a teacher in a school. One night she dreamt that she was riding home from school on her bicycle and when she was crossing a bridge she heard a voice: 'This is where your friends live.' The dream was so realistic that on one of the following days she acted on it. She rode the same way, found the bridge exactly as she had seen it in her dream, and there was a chapel of the Christian Community. The same priest she had experienced several years before in a different town stood at the altar. When the priest turned to offer communion to the congregation she saw that spiritual gold flowed from the altar to everyone who received the sacrament of bread and wine. This experience was decisive for her recognition of what actually takes place in the Act of Consecration of Man. For the rest of her life this woman connected herself with the Christian Community. I brought her communion on her deathbed and, together with her, I was able to experience the strong presence of the Third who was in our midst.

In Peru, where relatively many people still have remnants of clairvoyance, one of the local people said to my colleague, 'In the Act of Consecration of Man you people bring our gold back to us,' alluding to the looting of gold by the Spanish conquistadors. After the service the aura of the town was to his observation permeated with this gold.

This range of experiences from different times and in different churches perhaps shows that the presence of the Risen One is not limited to one period or one place. We don't need theology to recognise this. Humanly speaking, it probably takes no effort to imagine how Christ views all those different churches, times and circumstances. He does not look for dogmas, doctrines, fixed forms and norms. What is of essential importance to him is the reverence, faith and concentration human beings bestow on him. Then he can come to manifestation.

Diversity in unity

To recognise the newness of the Act of Consecration of Man relative to the past it is helpful to compare it with the Latin mass. This comparison soon shows that the Act of Consecration makes no radical break with the former liturgy, but is a metamorphosis of the old mass. Rudolf Steiner said to the priests of the Christian Community, 'The Act of Consecration of Man relates to the mass as the transformation that continues what is valid in the old, but has adopted the form that in our time flows from the spiritual world.'

The correspondence is recognisable also to 'outsiders', even to critics. For instance, Karl Bernhard Ritter, a critical Catholic theologian, who was a scholar of the history of liturgy, once wrote, 'The angels, who in the view of the Christian Community inspired the Act of Consecration of Man, must have been thoroughly familiar with the Catholic mass.'[2] Although the remark was made cynically, it is also correct; for the angels who inspire the sacrament the words are recognisable. The source of inspiration for the sacraments is the spiritual world, not human considerations.

In 1921 Rudolf Steiner made a free translation of the Latin mass for Hugo Schuster, a priest of the Old Catholic Church, so that he could work with this text in meditation and prayer. To another priest of the Catholic Church, who had asked him for a meditation, he gave the following instruction:

> Immerse yourself in the course of the day in the four parts of the mass:
>   1. *Gospel Reading:* with which you have to imagine that through this 'God's Word' comes to human beings for the intellect.
>   2. *Offertory:* with which you have to imagine that you voluntarily bring what you have as God's being within you, as an offering to God.
>   3. *Transubstantiation:* with which you have to imagine that the human element that is offered, is transformed into the truly divine.
>   4. *Communion:* with which you feel united with God.[3]

The Catechism of the Catholic Church does not speak of four parts in the mass, but limits itself to the two parts that were handed down by tradition from early Christianity:

> The liturgy of the Eucharist follows a fundamental structure that has been preserved through the centuries to our day. It unfolds in two great parts that form an essential content:
>   1. The *Liturgy of the Word* with the readings of holy scripture, the homily, and the intercessory prayer.
>   2. The *Liturgy of the Eucharist* with the consecration and the communion.

Here we recognise the classical two parts, the first one which people who had not been baptised could also attend; and the second one with the mass for the faithful.

At first sight it is easy to see why the Act of Consecration of Man selectively transforms parts of the old mass, and does not use other parts. The Latin mass consists of 41 parts. In the Act of Consecration we find parts 10–11, parts 13–15, parts 19–30 (a large part of the transubstantiation), and parts 34–38. We recognise in the Act of Consecration the pre-mass prayers that are spoken at the foot of the steps to the altar. The epistle (seasonal prayer) that marks the festival seasons appears in the old mass in one spot. In the Act of Consecration it is read both at the beginning and at the end of the service. It creates the possibility to move out of the experience of the temporal (seasonal) prayer and enter into the timeless reality of the ritual – and back again into the here and now. Together with the so-called pre-mass prayers we come to seven parts:

1. Pre-mass
2. Epistle
3. Gospel reading
4. Offertory
5. Transubstantiation
6. Communion
7. Epistle

Each of the seven parts is introduced by the sign of the cross on the forehead, the chin and the chest. Again, a comparison can illustrate where the differences are.

In early Christianity the sign of the cross was only made on the forehead. In the eighth century a second sign of the cross, on the mouth, was added to the first one. Not until the twelfth century was the third sign made, the one on the chest. This last sign is also called the German Cross; it spread especially in Central Europe.

Thus this sign slowly but surely descended, as if it came down deeper and deeper into the human constitution. We may imagine that this development reflects an increasingly close connection of the human being with the earth. In the Latin mass the Trinity is named when the cross is made: *'In nomine Patris et Filii and Spiritus Sancti.'* In the Act of Consecration of Man the threefold sign of the cross is made on the forehead, the chin and the chest – now however, the accent is placed on the activity rather than the name of the Trinity: 'The Father God be in us, the Son God create in us, the Spirit God enlighten us.'

As each part is begun with the signs of the cross, so each part is concluded with oft recurring words in the form of a blessing. Here also it is interesting to explore the correspondence in diversity and formulation.

In the Latin mass the priest turns eight times to the congregation with the blessing: *Dominus vobiscum,* 'the Lord be with you,' and the server answers each time: *Et cum spiritu tuo,* 'and with your spirit.' We find this greeting for the first time in the Old Testament, when Boaz greeted the reapers of the harvest with the words, 'The LORD be with you!' The reapers answered, 'The LORD bless you!' (Ruth 2:4). Evidently this mutual greeting played a role in the ritual customs of the harvest. We find a similar greeting in Psalm 129:8, where the reaper and the binder of sheaves say to each other, 'The blessing of the LORD be on you; we bless you in the name of the LORD.'

In the Act of Consecration of Man the celebrant similarly turns to the congregation eight times with a blessing gesture. The words that are then spoken are a metamorphosis of the classical blessing, 'Christ in you.' The server responds to this with 'And may he fill thy/your* spirit.' The change in the preposition from 'with' to 'in' indicates a world of difference.

We see something similar in the Christian Community in the transition from the Children's Service to the Confirmation and then to the Act of Consecration. For the children the preposition 'with' is still the right one. The celebrant addresses each child individually with the words, 'The spirit of God will be with you, when you seek him.' In the Confirmation, which takes place around a child's fourteenth year, sounds a different phrase: 'The Christ-Spirit be with you.' In the Act of Consecration this blessing turns more inward with the words mentioned above: 'Christ in you.'

A child who had received Confirmation expressed this transition in the following poem:

> Thirteen years behind me,
> My childhood will never come back.
> A short way completed,
> A long way to walk –
> To find a leader in yourself.
> Then only can you say:
> I am grown up.

---

* There are some small differences in translation between the wording in Britain and in other English-speaking countries.

You could call the Act of Consecration of Man the sacrament for grown-up Christians. In humanity's 'childhood' direction came from outside and from above. The Ten Commandments eloquently testify to this. As Christianity developed the emphasis shifted increasingly to the voice of individual conscience. In spite of countless efforts to restore the old commandments to their position of highest authority, in our time that does not work any more. The human being who speaks and acts out of his personal conscience becomes credible. This becomes possible by what Rudolf Steiner once called 'the Christ voice of human conscience.'

Something completely new in the history of liturgy is the content of the 'epistle' (literally 'letter') in the Act of Consecration of Man. The term comes from the mass, where there is a reading from the letters of St Paul. The Act of Consecration has at its beginning and end a seasonal prayer, a text in which the character of the festival season is expressed in a completely new manner. More than this, the epistles give an answer to the question of how Christ, in the Second Coming, works in the course of the year. Through these epistles a recognisable structure becomes visible in the sequence of the different parts of the Act of Consecration:

1. Epistle (seasonal prayer)
2. Gospel
3. Offertory
4. Transubstantiation
5. Communion
6. Epistle

When you come from the everyday world of space and time, The Act of Consecration first goes through the gate of the seasonal prayer, and then enters into the realm of 'the widths of space and the depths of time' (a term from the Offertory). After the four principal parts we come back to space and time with the concluding seasonal prayer. Thus this prayer forms the gate between the here and now and the dimension of the Spirit. Participants in the Act of Consecration can frequently sense that they come into a different experience of time at the altar. After the close you can sometimes have the impression as if you have been at the altar for an eternity, whereas sometimes it seems that the three-quarters of an hour of the Act of Consecration passed in the twinkling of an eye. Be that as it may, the experience of time is not to be compared with the hectic time pressure that usually pursues us.

To conclude this chapter we will compare some specific elements and formulations of the Latin mass and the Act of Consecration of Man. This will make the idea of the 'renewed mass' more concrete.

1. The Gospel Reading

In the preparatory text to the Gospel Reading the Latin mass evokes a picture from the Old Testament: 'Purify my heart and my lips, almighty God, who purified the lips of the prophet Isaiah with a burning coal.' It is the picture of the calling of Isaiah (Isa.6:6f), who could only become a prophet after one of the Seraphim had purified his lips with a burning coal from the heavenly altar. While in the Catholic mass the Father is addressed, in the Act of Consecration the priest addresses Christ with the entreaty: 'My heart be filled with thy/ your pure life, O Christ. From my lips let flow the word purified by thee/you.'

The drastic Old Testament picture of the calling of the prophet is Christianised and turned inward in the Act of Consecration.

2. The Offertory

In the Offertory of the Act of Consecration of Man we also see a more inner act of offering. In the early Christian church the faithful brought bread, wine and other offerings to the altar. Ever since the seventh century the priest has brought the bread himself. In the transition from the eleventh to the twelfth century the collection of money became practice; it took the place of contributions in kind. The Offering in the Act of Consecration does indeed have a connection with the raising of the chalice with water and wine, but throughout the Offertory and the subsequent Transubstantiation it becomes clear that the important point is the offering of thinking, feeling and will, the gifts of our soul. In the Transubstantiation the offering of Christ himself joins with the gifts offered by human beings.

In the Latin mass the offering gifts of bread and wine are accompanied by the silent prayer *(secreta)* of the priest. Later new offering prayers were used that are expressions of personal devotion. In the Western Church, unlike in the Eastern Church, prayers in the first person singular arose, which were sometimes addressed directly to Christ. In all places where in the Latin mass the first person is used we witness later developments. Although this begins as early as the ninth century in Spain, France and Ireland, Pope Pius V only officially confirmed these prayers in 1570. In the Act of Consecration we see a continuation of this individualised form of prayer in the Offertory and Transubstantiation.

3. The Transubstantiation

An example of the inward movement in the Act of Consecration of Man is the passage with the words spoken over the offering: 'thinking in purity, hoping for salvation, working from Christ.' In the corresponding passage of the Latin mass the words are (translated): 'this pure offering, this holy offering, this immaculate offering.' Once we have recognised the inward movement we frequently find it in diverse formulations.

When we compare the formulations in the actual transubstantiation we see another notable difference. The Catholic Church teaches that the transubstantiation takes place immediately after the words: *Hoc est corpus meum,* 'This is my body'.* By contrast, the Eastern Church views the transubstantiation not as a momentary event, but as a process, which begins with the words, 'This is my body' and reaches its culmination with the *epiclesis,* when the Holy Spirit is invoked. When the paten with the bread, and the chalice are raised, a prayer is spoken to the Father that the Holy Spirit may connect with these offerings. St John of Damascus *(c.* 675–749) wrote in his book *Exposition of the Orthodox Faith:*

> In the beginning God spoke, 'Let the earth bring forth green plants.' Even today the earth brings forth her vegetation, grown and strengthened by divine command, refreshed by rain.

* The magician's words 'hocus pocus' were probably derived from *hoc est corpus meus.*

Thus God also said, 'This is my body.' ... To this new planting the overshadowing power of the Holy Spirit is added as rain by the invocation [*epiclesis*].

In the Act of Consecration we recognise the process of transubstantiation in three phases, expressed in the words:

1. 'Take with the bread my body.'
2. 'May Christ hold sway in the bread that bears salvation ...'
3. 'Let the bread be Christ's body.'

The three statements describe a way from outer to inner, a process that penetrates progressively more deeply into the substances of bread and wine, until they are the body and blood of Christ.

Whereas the old mass more or less literally quotes the tradition handed down of the Last Supper, in the Act of Consecration a further development of this meal is described. St Luke described that after the words spoken over the bread and wine Jesus Christ told the disciples, 'Do this in remembrance of me.' The Greek word used here, *anamnesis,* means literally making something part of your inner world again, re-membering. Accordingly the words in the Latin mass are: *in mei memoriam,* 'in remembrance of me'.

As was mentioned before, in 1919 Rudolf Steiner made a translation of the Latin mass into German for Hugo Schuster, a priest of the Old Catholic Church. He freely translated the above words as follows (translated into English): 'And as often as you shall do this, take me into your thoughts.'

The Act of Consecration follows on this path with the words, 'Take this into your thinking.' In the subsequent passages this approach is developed further. From the wording it becomes evident that the human being is called to activate and enliven this thinking: 'And so live in our thoughts the new confession.' Finally, this process ends in an objective thinking that expresses itself within the human being: 'Thus thinks in us Christ's suffering and death.' This is an expression for the Christened memory that becomes pure thinking within us.

4. The Communion

The last part of the Latin mass shows a development similar to that of the offertory in that since the period between the ninth and eleventh centuries a number of prayers have been said in the first person singular. These new forms came into being in personal devotion (expressed in the Private Mass, a mass without congregation). In the Act of Consecration of Man, however, the I-form is no longer reserved for the priest, but every person in the congregation participates in it – it is not exclusive but inclusive. The I-form is present in the Communion from beginning to end. No longer is the communion of the chalice a matter for the priest only but, as was the original practice in the sacrament, bread and wine are shared by all communicants.

The way through the four parts of the sacrament goes from heaven to earth, from spirit to matter. In the four parts communion takes place in different ways.

The first part, with the Gospel Reading, creates a spiritual communion; the human spirit is addressed by the Spirit of Christ.

In the Offertory, where the powers of the soul are addressed, a communion takes place in the realm of the soul. The soul becomes 'enthused' and connects with the reality of the spirit. ('Enthused' comes from Greek *en* (in) and *theos* (God): 'God-filled'.)

The third part, the Transubstantiation, makes an appeal on the life or etheric forces. In the wording of this part we can hear that a deeper stream of life processes is being addressed that expresses itself in rhythm and repetition.

Finally, in the fourth part, the Communion, spiritual reality comes to expression in the substances of bread and wine. Only here does the communion become physical reality.

10

The Senses in the Sacrament

The altar service is a work of art that calls on all the senses, provided that we make them sensitive to the images and impressions that come from the altar. A connection with archetypal images, which have their origin in the heavenly ritual, grows through the images of the ritual. The original meaning of the word 'symbol' indicates this. The Greek word *syn-ballein* is 'to throw together', in other words, the visible picture of the symbol coincides with the archetypal image. The Dutch author, Gerrit Achterberg, had something similar in mind when he wrote, 'Symbols become cymbals in the hour of death.' When we die we will not only see 'face to face' (1Cor.13:12), but symbols become sounds that cut to the marrow. We are no longer outside them.

In our daily lives we constantly take in sense impressions. Only, our everyday sense impressions are usually not nourishing, but exhausting, destructive or even poisonous. Some impressions are burned into us, so to speak. The images we absorb can either have a traumatic or a healing effect.

In the ritual, sensory images give us the potential to develop. Slowly they can bring us closer to spiritual reality. St Paul indicated this gradual transformation with the words:

So the revealing light of the Lord is reflected in us all who have
unveiled faces. And we become transformed into the image
that we see, from one stage of clear shining-power to another,
shining in the light that rays out from the Lord who is the
Spirit. (2Cor.3:18).

Thus he said that we become metamorphosed into the archetypal image from one revelation to another. The sacrament leads us step by step in the direction of the archetypal image.

In this chapter we will focus on the role of the senses in the ritual of the Act of Consecration of Man. Actually, the Act of Consecration makes an uninterrupted appeal to our senses. It would impoverish the experience of the ritual if we would close our eyes all the time. It is better to be present, open and receptive. A street sweeper once said to Martha Heimeran, one of the founders of the Christian Community, 'I sit down for the Act of Consecration the way someone else sits down in the sun.' That is an apt way to describe a receptive presence.

All senses are portals to physical reality. In the Christian ritual the senses can become portals to true reality, because behind the outer images stands spiritual reality. The word 'portal' implies the possibility to open or close it. We need those abilities. If our senses were open and receptive all the time we would run the risk of being deluged by outer reality. But the other extreme also harbours a danger. Just imagine if we constantly mixed our own ideas in with what we observe; we would then run the risk that our perceptions become distorted. Clear observation always means active receptivity and receptive activity. If we try to follow the Act of Consecration only with extreme concentration we would end up in a kind of cramp. But if we only passively surrender to the sense impressions, without actively working with them inwardly, we run the risk that our attention will flag. True perception arises when there is active interplay between the observer and the object.

In early Christianity the senses also played an important role. Christ himself showed his disciples a new entry to reality by means of the senses. He emphasised that it is not appropriate for Christians to close their eyes to visible reality. Whereas eastern spirituality called the outer world maya (illusion), Christ showed the way to true perception:

> The light of the body is your eye. And when your eye is clear
> and pure, the life of your whole body will be illumined; but if
> your eye is clouded, then the life of your body, too, will be full
> of darkness. Therefore take care that the light is not turned into
> darkness in you. And when your body is completely illumined
> so that there is no room for darkness any longer, then there will
> be a shining radiance in you, as if a bright light shines within
> you. (Luke 11:34–36).

Actually, the Greek text does not read 'bright light' in the last line, but *astrapē,* the much stronger 'flash of lightning', as if to indicate free, open-minded observation. And in the second sentence 'clear and pure', is from the Greek word *haplous,* meaning open, sincere. The parables Christ used were mostly built up from such open, sincere observation.

Christ's appeal to our hearing is even stronger. Hearing is preeminently the religious sense organ: 'Whoever has ears to hear, let him hear!' and 'Pay heed to how you listen' (Luke 8:8,18). Out of a deepened, quietened listening faith can be born. In such listening what counts is not only the content of the words, the message, but also the tone. Countless times Christ tells us that we can recognise him by his voice. In the parable of the good shepherd alone (John 10:3–8) this motif occurs five times: the sheep hear, recognise and follow his voice.

This is an important point to find access to the Gospel, prayer and the sacrament. Can I try to imagine how these words sound when Christ speaks them? Can I let him speak the Lord's Prayer word for word? How do the words spoken over the bread and wine sound from his mouth? If we want to practise this we have to pause between the petitions of the Lord's Prayer and between the sentences of the gospel, so we can really listen. It is even more effective to walk around for days with one sentence from the gospel, put it 'under our pillow', and use it like a compass for daily life.[1]

Seeing at the altar

Any subjective judgment or emotion will cloud the reality of what we see. For this reason, in the quotation from Luke the word *haplous* is used: 'When your eye is open, sincere, the life of your whole body will be illumined.' We know the expression that someone is 'in a blind rage', or that 'love makes blind'. We know that fear can distort our observation. We have to try and contain all such soul movements, and transform them to perceive what is actually there.

Luke goes beyond a comparison of the eye with a clear lens that transmits light. Christ said to his disciples, 'The light of the body is your eye.' In other words, the eye is more than a clean, clear lens. The eye can become a source of light that lights up the body, 'as if a bright light shines within you.' This inner light, the light of insight, is like a bolt of lightning.

What does this mean in practice for the ritual? For instance, we might try to concentrate on the colours at the altar. We can look quietly at the colour, exploring it, as it were. Or we could explore the colours in their mutual contrasts. It is useful to close the eyes from time to time, and let the sense impression 'resonate,' in order to listen to an inner answer, as it were, when you see the colour. For we not only know the colours, but also their after-images, the complementary colours. And we not only know the mood of a particular colour as we see it outside us, but also the mood of the soul. This resonance is an important factor on the path of schooling. In his book *How to Know Higher Worlds,* Rudolf Steiner described in the chapter about conditions for the path of schooling the following:

> The world around us is filled everywhere with the glory of God, but we have to experience the divine in our own souls before we can find it in our surroundings.
>
> As students of occult knowledge, we are told to create moments in life when we can withdraw into ourselves in silence and solitude. In these moments, we should not give ourselves up to our own concerns. To do so would lead to the opposite of what we are striving for. Instead, in such moments, we should allow what we have experienced – what the outer world has told us – to linger on in utter stillness. In these quiet moments, every flower, every animal, and every action will disclose mysteries undreamed of. This prepares us to receive new sense impressions of the outer world with eyes quite different than before.
>
> If we seek only to enjoy – consume – one sense impression after another, we will blunt our capacity for cognition. If, on the other hand, we allow the experience of pleasure to reveal something to us, we will nurture and educate our cognitive capacities.[2]

The importance of the 'resonance' is brought to light in this passage.

After working with an impression in this way the possibility arises to take a new look, to observe the same object with different eyes and to deepen the impression. We can practise this capacity with all the elements of the Act of Consecration of Man. The forms, the light, the colours – but we shall see that a similar breathing in and breathing out is also possible with the other sense impressions.

Hearing in the Act of Consecration of Man

The motif of hearing runs like a continuous thread through both the Old and the New Testament. We find words 'hear' or 'hearing' appear almost 600 times in the Bible. It is the key to religious experience. I will illustrate that with the aid of texts from the Old and New Testaments, and then explore how hearing can be cultivated in the Act of Consecration.

The religious history of the Jews is unthinkable without the faculty of hearing. The Jewish people who were not allowed to make themselves an image of the Godhead, received as the first and greatest commandment: 'Hear, O Israel: The LORD our God is one LORD; and you shall love the LORD your God with all your heart, and with all your soul, and with all your might.' Then the people were told how they had to imprint this commandment into their memory, day and night. 'And you shall bind them as a sign upon your hand, and they shall be as frontlets between your eyes. And you shall write them on the doorposts of your house and on your gates.' (Deut.6:4f,8f) To this day each doorposts of a Jewish house has a *mezuzah*, a little scroll with this commandment in a container. At prayer times orthodox Jews wear *tefillin* – little boxes containing the commandment on a scroll that are attached to leather straps – on the forehead and on their arms, thus keeping the commandment literally. Religious life in orthodox Judaism is inconceivable without hearing.

With Christ, hearing becomes more inward with a prayer that is 'written in your heart.' No longer is the outer commandment decisive, but inner listening, as Luke said, 'Pay heed to how you listen.' This is something that we can use in the Act of Consecration. Pay heed to how we listen – with what intention, with what disposition.

We find the motifs of hearing, seeing and touching as 'religious senses' in the First Letter of John (1:1): 'It was from the Beginning. We have heard it, we have seen it with our eyes, we have beheld it and touched it with our hands: the divine Word which bears all life within itself.'

The statement from this eye-witness and 'ear-witness' of Christ begins and ends with hearing. 'We have heard it, we have seen it with our eyes, we have beheld it' *(etheasámetha)*. This word indicates more than outer seeing; it is a form of spiritual beholding, encompassing all the senses, as is clear from the last part: 'and touched it with our hands: the divine Word that bears all life within itself.' St Paul also makes the connection between religion and hearing clear with the words, 'Faith is born out of hearing' (Rom.10:17). By listening we deepen our faith.

The Act of Consecration of Man, however, does not begin with a sound impression, but with a visible image. First there is the picture of the server who comes in to light the candles. With the entry of the priest we hear a sound: three times the tinkling of the little silver bell.

A child who was prepared for confirmation and attended the Act of Consecration for the first time, experienced differing qualities in his hearing. 'In the beginning it is quiet, but there is still movement. Then it becomes completely silent, and later it is more silent than silent.' He used three expressions to indicate qualities of silence. The Greek language has two words for qualities of silence: *siōpaō* and *sigē*. *Siōpaō* means not-talking, outer silence. The other expression for being silent, *sigē*, occurs for instance in the Apocalypse: 'there was profound silence in the spiritual world, lasting for half a cycle of time' (Rev.8:1). The word *sigē* is sometimes translated as 'holy silence.' Maybe we could say that in the Act of Consecration silence develops from *siōpaō*, not-talking, to *sigē*, holy silence.

This is also what St Paul meant with the enigmatic statement: 'It is not right if the feminine speaks out in the congregation' (1Cor.14:35). In his time, women still had the role in ritual situations of expressing feelings of mourning and joy at the top of their voices. It happened in a way that prevented deepened attention and inner silence *(sigē)*. Paul did not mean to impose outer silence on women once and for all, but he asked them to contain their outer lamentations and exuberant joy, so that out of holy silence *(sigē)*, new speech could be born in them.

I will now illustrate the qualities of silence and listening by a few situations from the Act of Consecration.

It is a familiar phenomenon that in the beginning of the service we listen differently than at its end. But we can also hear this in the speech of the priest. It is particularly noticeable when the epistle, the so-called seasonal prayer, is repeated at the conclusion of the service; the same words sound differently. Frequently we can also hear it in the music, that sounds differently.

Someone who had lived for years with the Act of Consecration heard a different nuance in the words 'Christ in you' every time they sounded in the service. She has tried to describe it in her own words:

When 'Christ in you' sounds for the first time, there is a feeling of reserve, of holding back: who am I, that this may become mine? The second time there is a feeling of wonder: will this really come to me? The third time, light breaks through; the sun rises. Fourth, fifth and sixth times: the light grows with feelings of consolation, encouragement and thankfulness. The seventh time, after the communion, comes fulfilment, and we hear jubilation in these words. The eighth time, at the conclusion, the words encompass the entire message of salvation, as it lives in the ritual.

To strengthen the qualities of hearing in the Act of Consecration we can do some exercises:

- Pre-hearing. The evening before, we can try to pre-hear a sentence we still have in memory. The next morning we bring this sentence with us to the service.
- A second exercise is that of speaking-listening and listening-speaking. There are parts in the Act of Consecration that invite us to speak them with the priest. Obvious examples are the Creed and the Lord's Prayer. By our inner speaking-listening we are able to make a contribution to the sacrament. We may also consciously refrain from this inner speaking, and try to listen as if it were the first time we attended the service. We can even try to listen as if it were the last time.
- To deepen the listening quality it is helpful to be in the space for some time before the service begins. In the previous

chapter I described that the Act of Consecration is already being prepared before the candles are lit. The angel of the congregation is already present. We can sharpen our inner hearing by listening to the quality of the silence for some minutes before the service begins.

Occasionally it is given to us to hear through the words who is actually speaking. For instance, prior to the founding of the Christian Community, when Rudolf Steiner demonstrated the Act of Consecration of Man, Joachim Sydow, one of the founders, experienced the following:

Rudolf Steiner never celebrated the Act of Consecration of Man himself, but – as he called it – he demonstrated it to us. In other words, he showed it to us in real words and gestures, but in such a way that it was a real ritual act. However, he pronounced the first four sentences with such primal power that we were profoundly startled. It is hard to say what the source of this power was. It was not the power of the voice or the emphasis, but it was as if every word released the spell of the spiritual content it encompassed ...

I felt that if it continues like this, the curtain will be torn and heaven will be revealed, and I won't be able to bear it. But presently the unheard-of intensity of the speaker diminished and did not return until the last sentence. It was as if Rudolf Steiner, in acknowledgement of our weakness, had come down a notch, as if he had wanted to show us just once what the Act of Consecration of Man actually always should be.[3]

What is it that sounds in and behind these words? In the next quote a participant in the Act of Consecration described that he experienced the other world only at the moment when he came back into the here and now:

I had not attended the service very often. Precisely at what point the experience began, I can't quite remember. Actually I should say: I can't tell you that I had an experience; that only happened when I slowly came back into the world again.

The more I came back, the more it surprised me, and the more
I saw that I was sitting in the service and realised the reality
of everything around me. That I had been away I noticed
only by my returning, during which I at first kept hearing
only heavenly music. This changed gradually into words of
the celebrating priest that sounded like heavenly music. And
finally, I had the voice and figure of the priest before me again.

Three different impressions of sound. In the spiritual world the
service sounds like heavenly music. At the return into the body this
changes into words sounding as if the service were sung. Finally, the
person is back on earth and hears what is spoken in the moment.
In, through and between the words the spiritual world can become
audible. We can practice this way of listening by focusing on pre-
hearing and after-hearing of the text in the pauses between the
sentences. What is happening in the moments when there is not yet,
or no longer, speech?

There are two moments in the Act of Consecration when we have
an obvious opportunity to do this, namely during the silent censing
after the Offertory, and after the Communion of the priest. These
moments of silence ask for our listening. We can experience something
similar in the resonance of the Act of Consecration, if afterwards we
remain for a moment in the empty chapel. Sometimes the resonance is
even stronger than what we experienced during the service.

Someone related, 'In the subsequent few hours I hear certain
rhythms from the Act of Consecration that keep on working in me,
and I notice that my breathing and heartbeat have changed.'

The rhythms and sounds of the Act of Consecration can make
themselves felt for a long time. If a certain text has made a profound
impression on us, it can happen that we hear the sentence when
waking up the next morning, as a priest described it in his diary: 'In
my dream I forcefully spoke the conclusion of the inserted Christmas
prayer, "Healing is through you." The next day this sentence still
reverberated during the service.' How do these sentences sound in
spiritual reality?

I am also familiar with this phenomenon when listening to music.
If I have been listening intensively at a concert, I will still hear the
music when waking up the next few mornings.

It is useful to practice two different ways of listening. We can try with great intensity to become part of the words, step into them, as it were. The other method is to let go of the impressions from time to time and let them come into you. Let the words speak to you. By going back and forth between these two forms of listening you can hear the same words in very different ways.

We are rarely, or never, all-ear. We are all familiar with the phenomenon of our own thoughts coming in between. How do we get hearing and thinking aligned? We could say, these days every human being has a 'yes-but-constitution'. As soon as we say 'yes', there are doubts or contradictions ('but'). We are not people all of a piece. In the Act of Consecration the task is to overcome the 'yes-but'. How can we bring our own thoughts, associations and feelings into harmony with what we are seeing and hearing?

Via a detour I will come to a few answers. Rudolf Frieling sometimes compared what takes place in the service with 'golden buckets'. Every word, every sentence is a 'container' for spiritual content. The buckets are always the same; but the content differs from day to day. The well-known words are no more and no less than channels for the spiritual content that flows through them. That is what Rudolf Steiner meant in a lecture for physicians and priests when he said, 'Sense-perceptible actions are performed, and spirit streams into the actions.'[4] The idea is not in first instance to achieve a complete understanding of the contents, but to co-celebrate the ritual as a stream. As the celebrant you also cannot stop at a word or sentence. As a co-celebrant of the service we can inwardly try to speak with the celebrant, so that we follow the stream. The 'buckets' (the words) are not the actual reality; the content that streams into them is what counts.

Another means of dealing with the flood of words and images is to take a single sentence from the service home and 'cherish' it for some time. These sentences and images lend themselves to being carried with you, to 'walking with you'. This could be compared literally with the peripatetic method that was practised in the ancient Greek philosophers' schools: while walking they developed thoughts. That thoughts and pictures rise up in us during the Act of Consecration, that have little or nothing to do with the sacrament, is almost inevitable. Some thoughts do not let themselves be pushed aside. In many cases it is more effective to make them part of the ritual act.

After all, the Act of Consecration is actually one great intercessory prayer – for all those present, for all true Christians, for the dead, for the 'life of the world'. In principle, everything can be part of this intercession. Instead of pushing away the thoughts that arise in us about people and situations, we can integrate such thoughts in the great altar prayer. In times of war or natural disasters I try, when celebrating the Act of Consecration of Man, to give the images I have taken in a place in the ritual act. There have been horrendous images that had been stamped into my retina, which I took with me into the service for weeks, and even months – until I felt an inner awareness that the intercession had made a connection with this reality.

Eating and drinking in the sacrament

Anthroposophical terminology makes a distinction between higher and lower senses. The lower senses take in physically tangible impressions (such as the senses of taste and touch). The higher senses (such as seeing and hearing) 'explore' the impressions figuratively. With our eyes we explore the contours and colours of the world around us, but with the senses of taste and smell the world penetrates deeper into us, even literally. The culmination of the sacrament, when the reality of the spiritual world is felt as closest to us, is connected with the sense of taste and touch in eating and drinking.

For some people it is not easy to recognise a connection between the most profound spiritual experiences and something as common as eating and drinking. And yet, this connection was made by Christ himself when he announced his Last Supper and his imminent death. The announcement was so radical, so offensive, that a number of followers turned away from him. Many translations, including the rendition of the New Testament by Jon Madsen, which is used almost everywhere in this book, do not adequately do justice to the radical character of this statement:

'I AM the bread of life. Your fathers ate the manna in the
wilderness, and they died. This is the bread which descends
from heaven. Whoever eats of it will not die. I AM the life-

giving bread which descends from heaven. Whoever eats of this bread will live through all cycles of time. And the bread which I shall give – that is my earthly body which I shall offer up for the life of the world.' Then the Jews argued among themselves and said, 'How can he give us his earthly body to eat?' Jesus answered, 'Yes, I tell you: If you do not eat the earthly body of the Son of Man and drink his blood, you have no life in you. Whoever eats my body and drinks my blood has life beyond the cycles of time, and I give him the power of resurrection at the end of time. For my flesh is the true sustenance, and my blood is the true draught.' (John 6:48–55)

Jesus deliberately used words here that gave offence. What was translated here as 'Whoever eats my body' was expressed in the original Greek with the words *trōgein* (to gnaw, chew) and *sarx* (flesh). One commentator said about this passage, 'The word *trōgein* intentionally sharpens the sting of the word, which hurts one's feelings.'[5] Not only is the Greek expression almost untranslatable, it is also 'indigestible'.

The answer of Christ's disciples shows how offensive these words were, 'These are hard and difficult words; who can bear to hear them?' (6:60) The word 'hard' is here a translation of the Greek *sklēros* (harsh, rough; 'sclerotic' is derived from it). Jesus also was fully conscious of the effect of these words, 'Jesus was aware that his disciples could not come to terms with this, and he said to them, "Do you take offence at this?"' (6:61). He used the word *skandalizō* here, as in 'Are you scandalised by this?' The Greek *skandalon* means a trap in which you get caught.

The Gospel of John repeatedly shows this connection of the highest with the lowest, of the spiritual with the material. It also appears in the prologue to this Gospel, 'And the Word became flesh' (1:14), where the same word, *sarx*, is used for flesh. Johannine Christianity evidently places a certain emphasis on this connection; the highest must not merely become spiritual awareness, but must also become 'embodied', part of our body.

But there is an important difference with the everyday experience of eating and drinking, which becomes evident in Jesus' words, 'For my flesh is the true sustenance, and my blood is the true draught' (6:55). He distinguishes everyday eating and drinking, after which hunger and thirst always recur, from the communion, which satisfies and refreshes. A copious meal may leave us with a feeling of emptiness, as someone once said, 'I ate and drank, but the part of me that was really hungry did not receive anything.' In our time, even more than in the past, we are familiar with a world of hunger and the appearance of satiety, whereas in actual fact we are left even hungrier than before. Rudolf Steiner probably referred to this when he said, 'In the future people will perish of hunger at overfilled tables.'

In early Christianity people used succinct, strong expressions for the communion that illustrate what truly nourishes and refreshes. The Church Father Ignatius of Antioch (c. 35 – c. 107), who paid for his faith with martyrdom, wrote about the communion as 'the elixir of immortality'. In the communion we receive a gift that connects us with the world of the resurrection. This distinguishes Christianity from pre-Christian religions which did not (yet) seek a connection with earthly reality, but rather tried to free themselves from it. In Christianity the spiritual must become 'flesh and blood'. That happens visibly and tangibly, in the sacrament of bread and wine.

What must it be like for Christ to have to appear in the communion every day again? In the moment of transubstantiation, every day anew, he unites his being with earthly substances, 'uniting his soul therewith', as it sounds in the Act of Consecration of Man. In innumerable locations on earth, in countless different churches where the sacrament of bread and wine is celebrated, this union takes place every day.

One impressive document of the relationship of Christ with his followers is the diary of the French mystic Gabrielle Bossis (1874–1950). From the age of 63, she quietly wrote down what Christ told her in many inspirations and dialogues. After her death these notes were published in multiple languages. Following are a few fragments that illustrate how concretely and literally we can imagine our union with Christ in the communion. Once she heard him say after communion:

I have given Myself to the people, who did with Me what
they wanted. I did that out of love. Now I give Myself in the
Eucharist. Again people do with Me what they want. I do that
out of love until the end, to the end of time. (19 July 1939)

In the next passage the initial motif of this section, eating and drinking as the most profound form of connection with Christ, comes to expression:

> Thank Me for all My hosts, yours to the end of the world,
> to the one of the Last Judgment – these hosts, given for you,
> for My dwelling close to you. I see that you unite yourselves
> with Me, as I saw My apostles at the Last Supper. I come to
> you with a heart that is as deeply moved as in that evening of
> Maundy Thursday. Do not be afraid of the word 'eating.' I
> put it in the Gospel. The word expresses the unity I want to
> have with you. Eat Me. Eat Me, all of you, without fear.
> (12 June 1941)

Here sounds between the lines the silent expectation that we too unite ourselves with him in the communion, that this uniting is mutual. Thus, after his communion with the bread, the priest in the Act of Consecration of Man says, 'Take me as thou hast/you have given thyself/yourself to me.' Our task is to give ourselves completely to him in the communion. It is the strong longing for union that enables us to truly receive the gift of communion and to value it at its true worth.

Christ not only longs for this union during the Eucharist but also well before:

> All night long I have waited for you in My Eucharist so
> that I could give Myself to you in the early morning. Why
> are you surprised? Do you believe in My presence in the
> tabernacle? Do you believe in my infinite love? Then make
> the connection. But when you wake up during the night, may
> your gaze be directed to Him who already longs for you at the
> moment of dawn. That will stimulate your love and open your
> trust in My power. (21 March 1946)

At the Last Supper already this deepest longing of Christ to unite himself with the human being comes to expression in peculiar words. In the description in Luke of the Last Supper, Jon Madsen's rendition says, 'I have waited with great longing to eat the Passover with you.' The Greek text says literally, 'I have longed with longing *(epithumia epethumesa)* to eat the Passover with you.' With the same infinitely strong longing he waits day in, day out for his followers, so that he can share his gift with each of them.

We could perhaps imagine the transition from Transubstantiation to Communion, from the third to the fourth part of the sacrament, as follows. In the Transubstantiation Christ himself takes communion; he takes bread and wine. We find something similar in the description in the Gospel of Luke that after the resurrection Christ ate fish and bread in front of his disciples. He took the substances in his hand and permeated them with his presence. This occurs in every true sacrament. Occasionally a person may become aware of it, but even the mere indication of this reality can be overwhelming. This was described by Rudolf Meyer, one of the founders of the Christian Community, when during the words spoken over the bread and wine he saw what was actually taking place.

> It was the first time that I was cautiously pulled across the threshold through the Transubstantiation during the Act of Consecration of Man. While I was lifting up the host, I saw how above my hands, moving, accompanying and permeating them, other hands of light. The same happened when I lifted up the chalice. At first I tried to explain it as an optical illusion, but the phenomenon recurred at certain moments and could not be erased from the Act of Consecration. I was deeply moved. I could not speak about it nor could I explain it. When I told Countess Keyserlingk what I had seen she said right away, 'That was the Christ. He wanted to tell you: my hands are your hands.'
>
> Such experiences, when they are real, have the characteristic that they do not pale over time, but they grow. Thirty-three years later this sacred experience had grown into the experience of the ubiquity of the One, who is actively present in the Transubstantiation.[6]

Christ embodies himself – we should take this word literally – in bread and wine. When we receive his sacrament, we have the task to spiritualise this communion again. In the Act of Consecration this sounds in the words 'What my mouth has received become spirit in my soul.' This intriguing, enigmatic sentence contains the trichotomy of body, soul and spirit. Evidently, not only we can eat and drink the communion, but we can also ensoul and spiritualise it.

Another place where, if we pay close attention, we find a physical and spiritual communion is the Lord's Prayer. This was lost in the English version, but the original Greek admits of two meanings of the sentence 'Give us this day our daily [*epiousion*] bread.' Exactly in the middle of this prayer stands the remarkable word *epiousion;* 28 other words come before it and 28 words after it. The word *epiousion* does not occur in any Greek literature, only in the New Testament. We can understand the word as derived from the verb *epienai,* which means 'coming to you, coming at you.' The sentence would then mean that we pray for the bread that is destined for us.

But the word *epiousion* might also be a combination of *epi* (above) and *ousion* (being). In that case what is meant is supersensory bread. Accordingly, there are two Latin versions of this petition. The oldest one speaks of *panis quotidianus,* the bread that comes to us daily. But the translation by St Jerome *(c.* 340–420), the Vulgate, has *panis supersubstantialem,* supersensory bread. Maybe Christ intentionally chose this word with a double meaning to make us conscious of a physical and a spiritual union with him and the Father.

At any rate, he can only reach his goal if he can unite heaven and earth, spirit and matter, in the 'marriage of the Lamb'. Not only is that the ultimate goal of his revelation, namely to create a new heaven and a new earth; in a nutshell, in every sacrament in which bread and wine are consecrated, he celebrates the marriage of heaven and earth anew, in order to prepare secretly the future creation in us. The German Protestant theologian Oetinger (1702–82) said that corporeality is the end of God's way. But corporeality as we know it is not the end of creation. Christ continues the creation in order to renew life through the dying earth existence.

The corporeality of a new heaven and a new earth is the end of the ways of Christ. It is the image of the future with which the Apocalypse ends.

The sense of smell

With the sense of taste, described above, and with smelling and touching we arrive in the part of the world of the senses where impressions usually work unconsciously or subconsciously. For instance, before we have consciously perceived it, a certain smell can take us far back into our childhood. One of my friends once visited the Japanese concentration camp in which he had been imprisoned as a child during World War II. Without appreciable emotions he looked around the place – until he smelled something. At the post office he received a little jar with starch paste to affix a stamp on a letter. Suddenly he was assailed by violent emotions, when the smell of the starch reminded him of the porridge he had eaten in the camp as a child. With the smell disconnected childhood memories came back to him – more strongly than with anything he had seen and heard.

The incident illustrates how deeply some senses impressions work their way into us, and how important it is to 'nourish' all our senses with healthy impressions. Negative and unhealthy impressions can have lifelong traumatic effects. We recognise that with impressions of violence, which have a tendency of being burned into our soul – but with impressions of the lower senses the effect goes even deeper because they are less conscious.

Rudolf Steiner spoke in relation to sense impressions of 'cosmic nourishment' when he described that with every perception human beings take elemental beings into themselves.[7] After death, during the review of life, these sense impressions transform themselves into spiritual beings. In Rudolf Steiner's description of this process it becomes clear how important the role of the human being is in this regard; by receiving and processing sense impressions we can help these nature beings in their further development – or we can turn them into destructive forces by our own negative thoughts and indifference.

It is not difficult to conceive that in silent, deepened observation in the ritual we absorb spiritual forces that nourish the senses and create the potential of further development through us. What we have absorbed during life 'in dark outlines, as in a mirror,' we will 'see face to face' after death (1Cor.13:12). But what for us still lies in the future is already complete reality for the Godhead. When we let the smoke of the incense rise in the Act of Consecration, we perceive the good scent. An occasional person is also able to perceive something of the specific quality of this scent. During the censing of the altar someone attending the Act of Consecration for the first time heard himself think, 'This is piety.'

In the Old Testament we find an occasional expression that shows that the Godhead perceives the 'inside' of the offering, the intention – no doubt even more strongly than the human being can perceive it. When Noah brought burnt offerings after the Great Flood, the Old Testament says, 'And when the LORD smelled the pleasing odor, the LORD said in his heart: "I will never again curse the ground because of man".' (Gen.8:21). Thus a single offering, brought with the right intention, can change God's mind!

We tend to think in terms of symbols in relation to the offering: as the smoke ascends, so do our thoughts and prayers to the spiritual world. But whoever is able to observe the spirit sees much more than symbolism. One of my colleagues once had to lead a funeral service. The family had great problems with the censing of the casket, and asked if that part could be skipped. My colleague needed all his persuasiveness to convince them that censing the casket was an indispensable part of the ritual. In the end the family reluctantly agreed to it. After the ceremony the widow of the man who had died told that she unexpectedly saw the soul of her husband during the ritual, being borne up by the rising smoke of the incense. Anyone who has clairvoyant impressions of ritual acts invariably sees the spiritual reality behind occurrences that to our everyday consciousness merely seem to be symbolic.

Of old it was therefore a matter of course that in all forms of white magic offerings with a 'pleasing odour' were brought. An incense offering works according to the principle of the power of attraction of what belongs together. White magic works with pure, selfless sense impressions and pleasing odours to invoke helping spiritual forces. Conversely, black magic works with the most nasty odours and other sense impressions, by means of which demons are invoked. Rudolf Steiner gave the following example of this:

There are smells in which outright infernal influences of such beings enter into us. If a human being knows this he develops a conception of how he affects his fellow human beings when he forces them to breathe in all kinds of abominable scents. With patchouli, for instance, he enables certain spirits of the worst kind to enter into people. It is one of the worst forms of black magic to act on people through smells.[8]

Although in our time we tend to pay little or no attention to such things, it is known that, for instance at the French court in Versailles in the days of Louis XIII, XIV and XV, political intrigue and the use of certain perfumes went hand in hand.

At any rate, we can work with the impressions of scents both for good and for evil. In this regard we cannot afford any naivety. Everyone who consciously works with white, grey or black magic knows this.

The sense of touch

With the sense of touch we have, in a certain sense, arrived at the bottom of the sense impressions. Touch is one of the most fundamental forms of making a connection with the surrounding world. In the sense of sight, the eye actually remains outside the reality. The ear can penetrate more deeply into the reality of the outer phenomenon. But with the experience of touch we are, literally and figuratively, in contact with reality. This is the reason why the communion in the Act of Consecration of Man ends with touch. Some members of congregations are able to tell that this touch stayed with them for days. With this touch – with the index and middle finger on the temple – we may be reminded of a description of the laying on of hands in the New Testament, when Christ assembled the children around him, 'And he caressed the children and blessed them, laying his hands upon them' (Mark 10:16). With this laying on of hands they received his blessing power, a power that stayed with them for the rest of their lives.

Rudolf Frieling, who owed much in his life to a very special laying on of hands, described this experience in an impersonal way:

A person looked up to his beloved teacher with great
reverence. He pondered his words in his heart, owing
profound knowledge to them. And yet, what left a much
deeper and lasting effect in his soul was when this revered man
once laid a hand on his head, – a physical touch, yet filled
with greater spiritual power than the most lucid exposition,
that forever remained imprinted in memory. A blessing force
for life.[9]

In this careful manner Frieling described the indelible impression
a laying on of hands by Rudolf Steiner had made on him. In the
laying on of hands, more than with words or symbols, a power can be
transmitted that remains an unceasing blessing.

Winged sense impressions

The key to the sacrament is in all circumstances the activity of the
senses. We have seen in the above sections that all the senses are
addressed, and that the world of the senses opens the door to a
spiritual realm lying behind it. However, this encompasses not merely
the so-called nature spirits or elemental beings who guide the physical
world. From ancient times it was known that all uplifting and health-
bringing sense impressions also connect us with the world of the
angels. The apocryphal Book of Enoch mentions the angel of fire, of
snow, of light, of the moon, of lightning and thunder. In brief, every
sense impression of nature connects human beings with hierarchical
beings. Ambrose of Milan *(c.* 334–97) wrote, 'The air, the earth, the
water, everything is filled with angels.'
Cardinal John Henry Newman (1801–90) used an eloquent picture
to indicate the reach of our sense observations. He asked us to imagine
each breath of air, each beam of light, each radiation of warmth, each
delicious impression as a hem of the garments of those who behold
God face to face. What would we think if we would suddenly discover
that we were facing a mighty being that was hidden behind the object
we were examining? The being may hide his form, but as God's servant
he gives to all visible things their beauty and perfection. The things are
no more than their garments, their ornaments.

We can take another step in our exploration of the importance of the senses in the Act of Consecration when we listen to the epistles (the seasonal prayers) and their descriptions of the world of the senses. In these epistles, which change for each festival time, nature becomes part of Christianity. The sun, fire, clouds, air, night, the world of the stars, twilight – all these impressions are deepened and become religious, Christian experiences of nature. Since the Ascension, Christ has been working in the realm of the life forces, the ether world. This is also the realm where the most elementary nature phenomena are revealed. When he lived on earth, Christ was able to heal countless people from their defects and illnesses by touching them. Deafness and blindness were healed when Christ touched the ear or the eye. After his death and resurrection the sacrament gives him the possibility now also to touch our senses and heal them spiritually.

I hear many stories from participants in the Act of Consecration of the ways in which active participation in this sacrament nourishes, strengthens and heals the senses. Since for many people this is not a 'face to face' awareness, they tend to use analogies to explain what they experience. A few descriptions may make this more concrete.

> When I have actively participated in a service I have the
> feeling that I have been immersed in a bath and come out of it
> refreshed.

> After an Act of Consecration I move differently. It is as if I
> walk on wings. [This was not a person who goes about with
> his head in the clouds, but someone who noticed as he was
> walking that heaviness and fatigue had left him.]

> During the past year I could feel the effect of the Act
> of Consecration down into the physical. In the service,
> the breath, the body warmth, the heart become organs
> of perception for the Christ Being. The impressions are
> condensed into 'clair-feeling.' [This description takes us into
> the border area between sensory and clairvoyant perception.
> In the next two experiences the visible and invisible worlds
> flow together.]

With the lifting of the hands during the offertory the impression arises that the angel of the congregation extends his hands from the other side.

The visible movement is completed by an invisible, but clearly perceptible, counter movement. A priest once observed something similar when he was kneeling during the words spoken over the substances of bread and wine:

When I am kneeling there a space grows above me. This empty space is then occupied by Christ himself, who takes bread and wine into his hands.

Again and again we find in such descriptions forms of an interplay between what comes from the human being and what meets him out of the world of the altar. Such experiences can occur especially in the mood in which activity becomes receptive and receptivity active.

Sometimes I compare the Act of Consecration irreverently with an iceberg: a little tip is visible, but the largest part of what is really there is hidden from the eye. Even just being conscious of this enables us to observe differently. The senses become religious, instead of analytical, critical and judgmental capacities, reverence, attention and devotion are cultivated in our observation. Everyday life shows us that many people these days have developed an overdose of analytical, critical and judgmental capacities – capacities that divide rather than unite. But the qualities of reverence, attention and devotion are often hard to find in social life. The conscious path of the schooling of the senses in the Act of Consecration also has the result that in the long run we develop a different relationship with the world in our daily life and work.

The sense of warmth

In the classical teaching of the elements warmth is the element that permeates all forms of existence. Warmth manifests itself not only physically and in our feelings, but also spiritually. This shows in idiomatic expressions, such as someone 'has a warm heart'.

We don't mean that the person is physically warm-blooded, but that they radiate soul warmth. And if people are enthused, their spirit is filled with glowing warmth. In the Act of Consecration we may experience these three forms of warmth. Physical warmth alone already goes through a remarkable process. I can best describe this by means of two experiences I have had.

Once in a while I had to celebrate the Act of Consecration of Man when I had a fever. At the end of the service, and in the subsequent hours and days, I noticed that the fever was gone. And on an icy cold winter day I had to celebrate in an unheated room; every breath and every sentence formed a little cloud coming out of my mouth. Whereas the temperature in the room was well below freezing I noticed that during the Act of Consecration I became warmer and warmer. This kind of warmth is of a physical, psychic and spiritual nature. With this warmth we build a bridge between matter and spirit, between the earthly ritual and the heavenly sacrament.

It is also the realm where we can reach the those who have died, and can even help them. In kamaloka, the time when the dead are confronted with the consequences of their earthly life, they go through experiences that have to do with cold and heat, not in a literal sense, but spiritually. It has always been known that through unselfish love we can reach and help the dead. 'Love is strong as death' (S. of S. 8:6).

In meditations for the dead, which Rudolf Steiner often gave to people, we frequently see the motif of love, which cools what is hot and warms what is cold:

> May my love be interwoven
> As my heart's offering
> In the sheaths that now surround you,
> Cooling all your heat,
> Warming all your cold.
> Live – love-upborne,
> Light-rayed-through – on upward.[10]

Warmth not only builds a bridge between matter and spirit, but also between the living and the dead. In the Act of Consecration the dead are addressed and invited to participate in the service. In this way we can accompany them and help them on their way through the spiritual world. From time immemorial, this has been an important aspect of countless forms of the sacrament.

The sense of movement

Rudolf Steiner spoke of the sense of our own movement, the sense through which we are aware of our own movements. After we have discussed aspects of this capacity I will also describe the movements and gestures of the priest at the altar. If we take in these gestures intensively we will notice that we come into inward movement with everything that happens at the altar.

The sense of movement plays a role in the three signs of the cross that are made at the beginning of each part of the Act of Consecration. With the thumb, index and middle finger of the hand (a classic symbol of the Trinity) a cross is made over the forehead, the chin and the chest, while the following words are spoken as a prayer to the Trinity:

> The Father God be in us,
> The Son God create in us,
> The Spirit God enlighten us.

These signs must not become cursory, thoughtless gestures. The more they grow into true petitions, made with deliberate intention, and the more we include everyone present in these petitions (the plural 'us' is used for good reasons), the more efficacious will this prayer be. What happens then may be compared with the surf that washes over the beach and, after the wave has retreated, leaves water behind in the ripples of the sand. If we consciously make the sign of the cross, the spiritual world can flow into the gestures and fill them. This is also the significance of the gestures the priest makes at the altar. Gabrielle Bossis, whom I have quoted earlier, heard during the blessing of the priest Christ speaking the words, 'He makes the sign. It is I who bless you.'[11]

In a similar manner we may imagine that the Trinity itself fulfills this threefold gesture. It strikes me that in the sevenfold repetition of these signs of the cross the Trinity becomes more and more present.

After the communion the gestures and the petitions are fulfilled – much more strongly than in the beginning of the service.

In the Act of Consecration there are two additional moments when the sense of self-movement is addressed. During the reading of the Gospel the congregation stands up. And during the communion the participating members stand before the altar. The fact that this standing is much more than an outer gesture sounds in the words of the server who, prior to the Gospel Reading, speaks the words, 'We lift up our souls to thee/you, O Christ.' Standing for the Gospel Reading is like an exercise for the moment when we will stand before Christ. In the Little Apocalypse he prepares this moment by his appeal to us:

> Be of wakeful spirit at all times, school your souls in prayer, so that you may become strong to live through all that is coming without being harmed, and to be able to stand before the revelation of the Son of Man (Luke 21:36).

When we realise that in the Gospel Reading and in the Communion Christ himself stands before us, the act of standing receives its full significance.

Much more than our own movements (in which, by the way, not only our sense of movement but also the sense of balance and the sense of I play a role) the gestures and movements of the priest come to expression in the Act of Consecration. In exceptional circumstances we can notice how deeply the congregation takes these movements in and lives into them. I was once present when a priest, with the chalice in his hand, almost stumbled while he stepped up to the altar. A visible and audible shock went through the congregation when this happened – a manifestation of how deeply everyone was participating in what was taking place at the altar.

When the celebrant kneels, we inwardly kneel too. In this way every gesture, every movement has its resonance in the congregation. It is part of 'worthily fulfilling' the sacrament. The gestures comprise in the most concentrated form all that the Act of Consecration wants to say. From a colleague who lay on his deathbed I heard that he, since he was no longer able to meditate the service as a whole, limited himself to living into the gestures. This brought him also to the quintessence of the sacrament.

In a certain sense the ritual substances also make gestures during the service. The chalice is lifted up and is set down again. The incense rises up in smoke. The smoke makes an impressive gesture: first it whirls up like a cloud. After the offering the smoke comes to rest and often forms delicate veils that move slowly through the space until they dissolve. That too is part of the movements in the Act of Consecration of Man that can be observed and followed.

The sense of balance

A number of the movements and gestures discussed in the previous section also involve the sense of balance. Not only in the gestures but also in content, the threefold signs of the cross in the Act of Consecration are a model of balance: the threefold cross with its vertical and horizontal beam; the places on the forehead, chin and chest that relate to the human being's thinking, feeling and will; the three petitions to the Trinity – all of this evokes perfect inner balance. When we live with the meaning and contents of the Act of Consecration of Man for a longer time, we come to the point that we are imbued with the working of the Trinity, and we learn to think in terms of the Trinity. We develop a feeling of balance between the world of the Father, which is the ground of creation, and the world of the Spirit, which frees us from heaviness – in other words, a feeling of balance between matter and spirit, heaviness and lightness, below and above.

Especially the Christ greeting evokes the sense of balance. This gesture, in which the right hand is raised in blessing and the left hand points down in a similar gesture, creates balance between above and below, front and back, inner and outer, right and left. What we see there in a gesture is then strengthened by the words, 'Christ in you'. Both the gesture and the words come out of the middle, and address the middle.

Many complementary movements and gestures in the Act of Consecration of Man also address the sense of balance. Entering into the sanctuary is balanced by leaving it; stepping up to the altar asks for stepping down from it. Am I able to accompany these gestures inwardly? Taking off and putting on the biretta; opening and closing the liturgy book; the ritual movements between the right and left sides of the altar – it all speaks a silent language that wants to be understood.

While in some churches the movements between left and right at the altar are jokingly called 'from Pontius to Pilate' and are no longer comprehended, this symbolism was already known in ancient Israel. The two pillars Jachin and Boaz that stood in front of the temple of Solomon, represented day and night, offering and receiving, giving and taking. In the sounds of these names alone, in the vowels and consonants, we can hear the qualities of the light of the day (Jachin) and the darkness of the night (Boaz). In this way every true ritual develops in a balance of offering and receiving. Once we are aware of this principle we will have no problem recognising why, for instance, in the Act of Consecration the Gospel Reading takes place on the left side of the altar. When we then inwardly participate in these movements between left and right, we gradually come into balance during the Act of Consecration. By intensively following these movements in the service we become 'balanced', not in the literal, but in the figurative sense of the word.

The sense of the word

The sense of the word, also called sense of speech, is the sense that enables us to recognise words. A Dutchman who attended a celebration of the Act of Consecration of Man in the Finnish language was deeply impressed by it, even though he did not understand the language and hardly understood what was going on. But the words, their sounds and rhythms, the way they were pronounced, enabled this person to recognise the essence even before he understood the meaning of the words. We can see the same thing with young children who begin to say words before they understand their meaning. In the Act of Consecration we can practise this sense of the word and speech and, in doing so, find a whole new way to enter into the ritual language. This demands our concentration on the vowels, consonants and rhythm of the words, in brief, on the mantric character of the language.

In an early esoteric lecture Rudolf Steiner said that in the course of human evolution ritual has developed from 'word mantra' to 'thought mantra':

Previously, communication with the divine spiritual world
could only be brought about by mantras, through the sound;
now, however, humans can open themselves to union with the
Christ power through the meaning-filled Word within. The
words that carry us up into spiritual worlds should be winged
messengers.[12]

Similarly, Steiner described the oldest forms of the Lord's Prayer,
for instance the Aramaic or the Greek version, as word mantras. In the
languages of our time this prayer becomes a thought mantra. Steiner
differentiated this distinction even further in a lecture about the
development of speech, in which he called the language of Atlantean
times 'will language'.

In the post-Atlantean era until the Greek cultural epoch
language had the character of a 'feeling language'; and our
current cultural epoch uses primarily a 'thought language'.[13]

This characteristic is easy to recognise in the development
of liturgical language. Although there are groups that tell their
followers to practise unintelligible mantras, such as in transcendental
meditation, for most people this way is no longer of our time. Such
age-old mantras do have their effects, but they give the practitioner
the feeling that he is groping in the dark. Thinking is a capacity that
is especially developed in our western culture and cannot be excluded;
rather, it has to be integrated into our religious, ritual and spiritual
acts.

The old sound and word mantras work on the human being.
The well-known mantra *aum* is endlessly repeated until, in a certain
sense, it leads a life of its own. By contrast, a thought mantra works,
word for word, not *on* but *in* the human being, because through it he
develops his own thoughts.

In the Act of Consecration of Man we still find a remnant of sound
mantras in old words and names such as I-o-anes, the Greek form of
John; Pontius Pilate, a name with a special meaning and history; or
the names of all the heavenly hierarchies that sound from the altar at
Christmas time.

It is easier to recognise the mantric character of language in the rhythms of the ritual language. During Passion time, the rhythm of the sentences in the epistle and in the inserted prayer seems to come to a halt. A falling rhythm expresses the arduous way through suffering and death. By contrast, at Easter time there are upward striving rhythms in the epistle and the insert. For celebrating this insert, Rudolf Steiner gave the instruction, 'Spoken with great devotion and warmth.' As during Passion time everything seems to come to a stop, so at Easter time everything begins to flow again in the liturgical texts.

If we concentrate for some time on this aspect of the ritual language, participation in the Act of Consecration will be enriched by experiences that take us into an entirely different world than that of thinking and understanding.

The sense of thought

When we communicate in our own language we are not focused on the sense of the word, or hardly so. What is much more important is the information we want to share with the other, and the relevant thoughts. When we hear a more or less unknown language, we focus on very different qualities of the language. It was for good reason that the old mass was celebrated in Latin for centuries. The mantric character of the language stimulated the sense of the word. The sense with which we can follow thoughts did not yet play a role in the old liturgical language.

This is different in the Act of Consecration of Man. No word, no sentence, no act need escape our thinking. While in the old mass the *sacrificium intellectus*, the sacrifice of the intellect, was necessary to gain access to this ritual language, in the Act of Consecration thinking is integrated; it forms part of the ritual speech and acts. This is noticeable in the words spoken over the bread and wine; the classical formula, 'Do this in remembrance of me,' was transformed into 'Take this into your thinking.'

We can practise the sense of thought in the Act of Consecration by comparing specific formulas. For instance, we might wonder why the celebrant sometimes speaks in the first person singular and in other parts in the plural 'we'. In addition, the word 'I' has a different meaning in different parts of the service. The offering develops from I to we: 'I bring it because to thee/you have also flowed my strayings from thee/you.' 'With me bring it all who are here present.' This movement from I to we is extended further by taking the dead into the offering. The celebrant also speaks in the I-form during the communion. But he does not receive the communion for himself, even though he speaks, 'I take the bread' and 'I take the wine'. Here the celebrant receives the communion on behalf of and with the congregation: the I has become inclusive.

Rudolf Steiner more than once used the word *ganzmenschlich* (fully human) to characterise the activity of the priest during the celebration. The priest must be present with all the faculties of the soul – with thinking, feeling and will. In the course of the Act of Consecration, thinking becomes pious. For that is the meaning of the sentence, 'Take this into your thinking.'

Just imagine if there would be no person on earth who still gives Christ a place in his thoughts; that there would be no one who knows of his existence; that there would be no prayers, no offerings, no ritual anymore on earth. Rudolf Frieling once compared this possibility (which today is no longer inconceivable) with the condition of a person who lost all of his memory and no longer knows who he is. The loss of Christ from our thoughts would be the most radical form of collective memory loss, coupled with total hopelessness about the future. We would not know anymore where we came from, who we are, and what our future is. In this context the drastic statement Rudolf Steiner once made to the priests becomes understandable, 'When there is no more ritual on earth, the potential to gain knowledge ceases.'

The sense of life

Comfort and discomfort, vitality and fatigue, stress and relief, are all expressions of our sense of life. All human beings, consciously or unconsciously, have a perceptive faculty for qualities of life, both in their own bodies and in the surroundings. The environment may be so empty and deadly that we have the feeling our life forces are being sucked out of us. Or a landscape may be so rich and alive that even just the view of it can have a regenerating effect.

The sense of life, however, is also a religious sense. We can immediately notice this in one of the best-known psalms (Psalm 23):

> The LORD is my shepherd, I shall not want;
> He makes me lie down in green pastures.
> He leads me beside the still waters;
> He restores my soul.

How is the sense of life addressed in the Act of Consecration of Man? Which qualities of life does it point to?

First of all, it is not about our own life or that of other people, but the human being turns with heart and soul to the pure life of Christ (a phrase from the text that introduces the Gospel Reading). In a similar way we can also consider the many life motifs in the Communion. In a certain sense there are three forms of communion in the Act of Consecration. In the words spoken over the bread and wine during the Transubstantiation, Christ unites his soul with the ritual substances. We might call this the communion of Christ. He unites himself with the bread and wine.

During the actual Communion the priest receives the communion, and finally the members of the congregation. In the communion of the priest it becomes evident that with the body and blood of Christ we also receive his pure life, when the priest says, 'The body of the Lord heal my soul, that it continue to live.' Here the Act of Consecration follows the view of the early Christians, who experienced the communion as *pharmakon athanasias,* the elixir of immortality.

Ignatius of Antioch, who used this formula around AD 117, continued the sentence with, 'that we may always live in Christ.' The communion is a gift for our life forces. Nowhere else are our life forces so nourished and quenched as in the communion. This is also a decisive experience in the spiritual communion with Christ: Christ is our life. Only by connecting with him do we truly come to life.

The French author Jacques Lusseyran, who was on the verge of death due to a serious illness in a concentration camp during the Second World War, wrote about this experience as follows:

> Have I said that death was already there? If I have I was wrong.
> Sickness and pain, yes, but not death. Quite the opposite, life,

and that was the unbelievable thing that had taken possession of me. I had never lived so fully before.

Life had become a substance within me. It broke into my cage, pushed by a force a thousand times stronger than I. It was certainly not made of flesh and blood, not even of ideas. It came toward me like a shimmering wave, like the caress of light. I could see it beyond my eyes and my forehead and above my head. It touched me and filled me to overflowing. I let myself float upon it.

There were names that I mumbled from the depths of my astonishment. No doubt my lips did not speak them, but they had their own song: 'Providence, the Guardian Angel, Jesus Christ, God.' I didn't try to turn it over in my mind. It was not just the time for metaphysics. I drew my strength from the spring. I kept on drinking and drinking still more. I was not going to leave that celestial stream. For that matter, it was not strange to me, having come to me right after my old accident when I found I was blind. Here was the same thing all over again, the Life which sustained the life in me.[14]

In our everyday, common life we are hardly justified to call ourselves alive. 'You have the name of a living being, yet you are dead,' says the angel of Sardis (Rev.3:1). Not until we unite ourselves with Christ, by eating and drinking him, do we really begin to live.

One of my colleagues heard Christ's voice as she was lifting up the bread at the altar: 'Are you aware that you have in your hands the most precious substance that exists in the world?' Most of the time we don't know this. Only the realisation that we receive Christ himself makes us worthy to receive communion.

The sense of I

With our sense of I we perceive the I of another human being. This capacity works according to the well-known principle: like recognises like. We have to mobilise our own I for this. Of course we also use other forms of observation to become aware of another human being, but with those we do not penetrate to the essential being of the other.

If we observe someone only in his physical appearance, we literally and figuratively just remain on the outside. If we are irritated by someone we only see the rigid patterns of our preconceptions, but we fail to notice what is unique in him.

In brief, by mobilising our sense of I we can create a different quality in encounters, which enables us to discover what is genuinely unique in the other. Personally, I have the impression that through the sense of I we enter a realm that we will consciously enter as we die. In the near death experience we can recognise this encounter of our I with the I of Christ in its purest form. All outer appearance dissolves. Then only do we recognise the One to whom we owe our life. George Ritchie described this perception of the I of Christ in his near death experience when, while he was out of his body, he saw an overwhelming light:

> 'I'm glad I don't have physical eyes at this moment,' I thought.
> 'This light would destroy the retina in a tenth of a second.'
> No, I corrected myself, not the light. He. He would be too
> bright to look at. For now I saw that it was not light but a
> Man who had entered the room, or rather, a Man made out of
> light, though this seemed no more possible to my mind than
> the incredible intensity of the brightness that made up
> His form.
>
> The instant I perceived Him, a command formed itself in
> my mind. 'Stand up!' The words came from inside me, yet
> they had an authority my mere thoughts had never had. I got
> to my feet, and as I did came the stupendous certainty: 'You
> are in the presence of *the* Son of God.'
>
> Again, the concept seemed to form itself inside me, but
> not as a thought or speculation. It was a kind of knowing,
> immediate and complete.[15]

The awareness of the I of Christ, when it happens, is so self-evident that our usually reasoning and doubting intellect is completely silenced. People who have had such an experience are once and for all cured of all doubts. They have experienced a world that is more real than the so-called reality of daily life. That is what Willem Zeylmans van Emmichoven was trying to express in the title of his book,

The Reality in Which We Live. That he was conscious of the impossibility to describe this reality is expressed in the first sentences of the book:

> At a certain stage of my development I came to the inner
> realisation that Christ is the reality in which we live. As I write
> this sentence, I am aware that it will hardly be possible to
> express all I mean by it.[16]

To become aware of this reality we need our sense of I. The same organ of perception is needed to penetrate into the Act of Consecration of Man, for in this service we stand before Christ. He looks us in the eye. When we stand before the altar, his eye rests on us. All that the priest speaks and does is in a certain sense a reflection of his speaking and doing. People who see him face to face at the altar can attest to this in many different ways, although it is always difficult to express it in earthly words.

One person wrote about this encounter, 'I beheld a figure of light who stretched out his hand to me. In place of the hand of the priest the hand of Christ appeared.' Christ acts in the acting of the priest. He speaks through the words spoken by the priest.

We can become aware of the fact that something very real happens with our feeling of self in the Act of Consecration of Man when we compare the awareness of the I at the beginning of the service with that at the end. In my own experience, I have noticed the following: in daily life our sense of I constantly swings back and forth between feelings of superiority, which want to place us above other people, and feelings of inferiority, by which we want to make ourselves smaller than others. These are the two shadow sides of the I with which we are confronted all the time. In the Act of Consecration it is as if these scales, which are continually moving up and down, gradually come into balance. Whereas at the beginning of the service we recognise these alternating feelings, as the service progresses a pure feeling of I starts to form, which is characterised by an awareness of being myself: this am I, no more and no less. I occupy the space that belongs to me. We could describe it as a feeling of poverty and wealth at the same time. This feeling culminates in the communion.

The fact that something extraordinary is happening here with the human I can also be heard in the words of the priest which he speaks after the communion of the bread, 'Take me as thou hast/ you have given thyself/yourself to me.' This is the encounter of I with I of which Rudolf Steiner said to the founders of the Christian Community, 'During the Communion the higher I of the human being is present.' In daily life our higher I is often far away, for it is not continuously connected with the human being. The I we make use of in ordinary life is a mere shadow of it – sometimes no better than a caricature. It is a kind of crutch we have to use. Compared with this everyday I, the higher I is our backbone. That the higher I is present in the Communion can also be noticed by the feeling that everything incidental and inessential falls away, and that we penetrate into our own core: this is who I really am.

11

Ritual and Visual Art

The farther we go back into the past, the more evident becomes the connection between ritual, art and science. In earliest antiquity all forms of culture still originated in ritual. In the course of time, art, science and religion each went their own way and grew apart. But in our time we may still have a vague feeling that something is lacking when someone occupies himself with only one of these three realms. We don't quite feel like complete human beings unless we have integrated these three realms in our lives to some extent, when thinking, feeling and the will are all involved.

Of course, science makes an appeal first of all on our thinking. Art has the potential of speaking pre-eminently to our heart. Religion is primarily a matter of will. Only later in the development of religious life do philosophies of life, dogmas and doctrines arise but, in essence, religion calls on the will life. That is the reason why in all forms of religion repetition of ritual acts plays an important role.

It wasn't until in Greek culture that art, science and religion first began to diverge. Before that time – for instance in the Egyptian, Ancient Persian and Ancient Indian cultures – they were still unified in the priests, priest-kings or pharaohs who determined culture in the ancient theocracies. In early Greece the archaic art was still fully interwoven with sacral life. Only later in Greek history do we see 'worldly' forms of art and culture. One example will illustrate this development from ritual to culture and art.

From ritual to culture

On the 'island of the gods' Samothrace, the island of the Cabeiri, a remarkable form of ritual was practised. The historian Herodotus (484–424 BC), who visited the island, related that so-called vessel-gods were standing on the altar of the temple of Samothrace; these were called the Cabeiri. These archaic divine figures belonged to the chthonic gods – they dwelt in the earth. Herodotus compared the Cabeiri with images of Hephaestus and with the Pataikoi from Phoenicia, lofty gods in the shape of dwarfs.[1] In the Louvre in Paris we can see a few Pataikoi from Phoenicia; they indeed look like strange pixies.

In antiquity these statues were kept in the dark Holy of Holies of the temples; as gods of the sub-earthly world, they were never exposed to daylight. Goethe brought the Cabeiri to the stage in the scene of Walpurgis Night in his *Faust* – Nereids and Tritons (gods of the sea) there carry a gigantic turtle shield on which three ceramic vessels are standing. The turtle shield is a symbolic representation of the earth, in which the Cabeiri live. The sea gods announce their arrival with the words:

> They're gods that we are bringing
> High songs must you be singing!

The sirens reply:

> Small to the sight,
> Great in their might,
> Saviours of the stranded,
> Ancient Gods, and banded.[2]

The Cabeiri may be 'small to the sight,' but they belong to the mightiest gods. They work in hidden realms. In *Faust,* Goethe called them, 'always further yearning, with desire and hunger burning for the unattainable.' They are not 'complete' like the Olympian gods, but they are connected with the becoming of earth and human beings. They are still developing. In this connection, Rudolf Steiner spoke of the Cabeiri as 'the guardians of forces connected with the genesis and further evolution of humanity,' especially the three with the names Axieros, Axiokersos and Axiokersa, who work out of the Trinity.[3]

The philosopher Schelling studied the Cabeiri intensively. Rudolf Steiner extended his observations and made them more concrete, resulting in the following picture of the Cabeiri cult. For a performance of the Walpurgis Night in *Faust* he designed three vessels, of which he said that they were artistic images of the statues of Samothrace, which were hollow.

In Samothrace glowing charcoal was put in the vessel, onto which incense was dropped. The priest spoke ritual words into the smoke that rose out of the vessel. There was a sacred language on Samothrace that was used only in these mysteries. When these ritual words were spoken into the rising smoke, for clairvoyant observation the figures of the Cabeiri appeared in it. A Greek proverb said, 'In the ascending smoke the gods descend.'

Here is the principle of the ritual act in the most elementary sense of the word. Three worlds come together in this one place at the altar:

- The smoke rises out of the vessel,
- The priest speaks ritual, mantric words into the rising smoke. (In Roman antiquity they were called mystic voices.)
- In the ascending smoke, permeated with the offering word, the gods are revealed.

This age-old ritual continues to be practised in our time when in countless liturgical forms incense is offered on the altar. In old pictures and in descriptions we find that in the sacrificial smoke the Godhead reveals himself to clairvoyant vision.

The above description indicates clearly where sacred images and ritual objects have their origin. Initiates originally 'saw' and 'read' the various forms of ritual in the spiritual world, which speaks in imagination, inspiration and intuition. Subsequently, the initiates 'translated' these spiritual images (imaginations) into visible forms, and they transformed the spiritual word (inspiration) into the liturgical word. We can follow this gradual development in the founding of the Old Testament rituals. On Mount Sinai, Moses, the initiate of the Hebrew people, received the instructions to serve the Godhead in ritual images, words and acts 'after the pattern for them, which is being shown you on the mountain' (Exod.25:40). Jewish culture, however, did not bring the divine to manifestation in visible sculpture. Right from the beginning on Mount Sinai

Figure 16. The three Phoenician Pataikoi. Louvre, Paris.

Figure 17. The three Cabeiri, designed by Rudolf Steiner.

one commandment in particular would govern Jewish culture, 'You shall not make for yourself a graven image, or any likeness of anything that is in heaven above' (Exod.20:4).

Christ and his image

This custom changed radically in Christianity. Christ himself initiated this change when he said, 'He who has seen me has also seen the Father' (John 14:9). With his coming to earth the unimaginable became imaginable, the invisible visible, the inaudible audible. This turning point in religious and ritual life was indicated in the words of the creed, *Homo factus est,* 'and was made man'. With Jesus Christ's coming to the earth, God became man. In musical representations of the Latin mass these words frequently mark a high point in the composition – for instance in Bach, Beethoven, Bruckner, and also others.

Still, the external appearance of Jesus Christ was not the most important aspect in the many encounters he had with people. We know that his words sounded 'as though all creative power [*exousia*] and the might of worlds [*dynameis*] were in him' (Luke 4:36). The earliest documents that give an impression of his outer appearance describe an inconspicuous figure. The Jewish historian Flavius Josephus wrote:

> In those days a man with a bewitching power appeared – if it
> is permissible to call him a man; some Greeks call him a son of
> the gods. His disciples call him the true prophet, who is said
> to have raised the dead and healed the sick. Both his being and
> his stature were human, for he looked like a simple man, with
> a dark complexion and narrow face, a long nose and eyebrows
> that had grown together, so that people who saw him could be
> put off. He had little hair that was parted in the middle of
> his head.[4]

It is not entirely clear whether this text was later altered or even added by others, but we find something similar in a description by Clement of Alexandria:

He did not have the beauty of outer appearance that is
based on an illusion, but true beauty in soul as well as body,
which in the soul consists in goodness and in the body in the
immortality of the flesh.[5]

The prophet Isaiah, who foresaw his coming, also described an
inconspicuous appearance: 'He had no form or comeliness that
we should look at him, and no beauty that we should desire him'
(Isa.53:2).

Only on one occasion Christ showed himself in his true form,
namely when he revealed his radiant splendour in the transfiguration
on the mountain. Luke used this word *doxa* in his description of this
event. He made an explicit connection between the *doxa* and the
transfiguration on the mountain:

And it was about eight days after these words that he took
Peter and John and James with him and ascended the
mountain to pray. And while he was still deep in prayer, the
appearance of his countenance changed and his garments
became gleaming, radiant white ... Peter and the others who
were with him sank into deep sleep. But when they awoke
they beheld the radiance of the spiritual light [*doxa*] that
shone from him. (Luke 9:28,32)

When after years Peter looked back on this event he used an
unusual word to indicate what took place on the mountain:

We did not follow thought-out ideas when we brought you
knowledge of the power of being and the spiritual coming of
Jesus Christ, our Lord. We spoke to you as those to whom
it has been granted to perceive the majestic revelation of his
being. From the Father God he received dignity of soul and
spiritual light when the voice spoke to him out of the exalted
revelation:
    'This is my beloved Son, in him have I revealed myself.'
    This voice we heard sound forth out of the heavenly heights
when we were with him on the holy mountain. (2Pet.1:16-18).

Peter was an eyewitness and heard what the Godhead spoke on the mountain. For beholding Christ's revelation he used for this occasion a word that came from the Greek mysteries. This word, *epoptes* (beholder, observer – in the quote: those who perceive) was used in the mysteries of Eleusis for the highest degree of initiation, when the initiate was able to behold (perceive) the Godhead face to face.

After his resurrection Christ appeared in 'holy sheaths', which is the reason why his followers did not immediately recognise him. When he appeared in his true form to a few individuals after his ascension (Paul before Damascus and John on Patmos) his appearance was again so overwhelming that they could not bear it. Paul was blind for a few days, and John fell at his feet as if dead.

For a long time after the beginning of Christianity the ancient laws that forbade making images of the Godhead continued to hold sway. In the Roman catacombs we find graffiti (in antiquity these were scratchings or paintings) with primitive, symbolic signs, but the Crucified One or the Resurrected One was not himself represented. The first image is a caricature of a crucified person with the head of an ass. This caricature was found on the wall of a military school in Rome and is from the first century. Beside the Crucified One we see a man who raises his arm. Under the picture are the words: 'Alexamenos worships his god.'

Not until the middle of the third century do people begin to make pictures of Christ. Before that time we find the symbol of the fish, the anchor, or the Christ monogram. There are earlier pictures of the good shepherd, of the raising of Lazarus, and other signs, but these depict the signs and do not represent an outer appearance.

In the course of time Christianity divided into the Eastern and the Western Church. In the East the picture of Christ developed into an archetypal icon: a picture of Christ that is not created by human hands. A legend tells that a ruler, Abgarus, received from Christ himself a sweat-cloth, a *mandulion,* with an imprint of the face of Christ. This *mandulion* was brought to Constantinople, and in 1204 it was taken by crusaders and brought to western Europe.

The legend of Veronica (etymologically perhaps a corruption of *vera icon,* true image), which arose in the Middle Ages, also tells that the image came from Christ himself. In eastern icon painting artists

Figure 18. Graffiti of crucified ass. Catacombs, Rome.

base themselves on Luke, the evangelist who was said to have been the first person to make an image of Jesus Christ. A characteristic of the art of icon painting is that it faithfully follows certain prototypes, and that a painter hardly adds anything original to it. It is a supra-personal, sacred art.

In western Christianity sacred art developed in a completely different way. What became more and more important in the course of its development was the artist's own imprint. Especially since the Renaissance, the concept and the technique and style of the artist played an ever growing role. The visible image became more and more a 'portrait', and the technique of painting was developed to great perfection. In the nineteenth century this image of Christ became mostly reduced to an aesthetic outer picture and even to kitsch.

This dichotomy between eastern and western Christianity corresponds with two biblical references to Jesus Christ. Eastern Christianity is oriented on the Son of God, while western Christianity puts the Son of Man in the centre.

In an Easter lecture Rudolf Steiner once described these two aspects of Christianity, both of which represent a one-sidedness, in their mutual interaction. He showed how western Christianity came to a dead end by focusing for centuries on the man of sorrows and the death on the cross. In the process, it gradually lost sight of the reality of the resurrection. True, the resurrection is inconceivable without the death on the cross, but the death on the cross without the resurrection is a senseless, hopeless end of life.

> Easter must become an inner festival, a festival in which we
> celebrate in ourselves the victory of the spirit over the body.
> As history should not be disregarded, we shall not ignore the
> figure of the pain-stricken Jesus, the Man of Sorrows, on the
> Cross; but above the Cross we must behold the Victor who
> remains unaffected by birth as well as by death, and who alone
> can lead our vision up to the eternal pastures of life in the Spirit.
> Only so shall we draw near again to the true Being of Christ.[6]

Steiner described the development of Christianity in the west as a movement that has dragged Christ down and has reduced him to 'the simple man from Nazareth.' He indicated that in the old mysteries the initiation consisted of two experiences. After the picture of the suffering Christ, with which the initiate had to identify himself, appeared the picture of Christ triumphant, the vanquisher of death.

This unity-duality appears in the altar pictures of the Christian Community. Rudolf Steiner indicated that these two images, that of the crucified and that of the resurrected Christ, should be brought into a unity in the altar painting. The priest and artist Johannes Rath, who made many altar paintings for the Christian Community in the 1950s and 60s, once spoke of a 'confession of impossibility', because for the artist it is a near impossible task to blend these so totally different elements into a unified picture. Once we have recognised this principle we find this unity-duality throughout the sacraments of the Christian Community.

As 'the most down-to-earth of all religions' (an expression of Rudolf Frieling), Christianity has the task of uniting two worlds with each other. Both the sobering, earthly reality of the death on the cross and the lofty, spiritual reality of the resurrection have their necessary place in this picture. In the celebration of the sacraments, if it is done right, this unity-duality, which we could call 'holy matter-of-factness', will also sound. If there is only the down-to-earth aspect, the service will have no 'wings'; but if the emphasis is only on holiness, the service has no 'roots'. Also the servers and the congregation have the task, as co-celebrants, of bringing this twofold connection to realisation.

In the search for appropriate images I have been led by the question of where does art make visible something of the spiritual reality behind the outer appearance of ritual and prayer. I shall limit myself to old pictures that are derived from the Old and New Testaments.

Earthly and heavenly ritual

When we on earth perform a ritual or say a prayer we call on the spiritual world. We may even turn the movement around: before ritual or prayer take place on earth the spiritual world is already working at the altar. When you enter the church where I regularly celebrated in the Netherlands, in which the chapel is one floor up, you come into the building below the place where the altar is standing. One of the members of our congregation, who is frequently able to observe the ritual clairvoyantly, described that before every Act of Consecration she saw how the angel of the congregation prepares the service. The angel was not only present at the altar, but also above and below it. Under the altar, his presence could be felt as a powerful, vibrant energy.

The reality of earthly ritual is a fragment of a greater reality which in ancient times was called the heavenly ritual. This heavenly ritual was painted quite concretely, yet gracefully by the Van Eyck brothers in *The Lamb of God*. The central part of the painting represents the altar in heaven on which the Lamb of God (Christ) is sacrificed, as described in the Book of Revelation:

> After this I saw: see, a great assembly which no one could count, from all people and tribes and races and languages. They stood before the throne and the Lamb, clad in white garments, with palm branches in their hands. And they called out with a great voice: healing is of our God who sits upon the throne, and of the Lamb! (Rev.7:9f).

Earlier the Book of Revelation had described that this divine Lamb had been sacrificed. (5:6) As one commentator described, the Van Eyck brothers pictured 'the heavenly ritual in an earthly paradise.'[7] The connection between earthly beauty and heavenly radiance can be found in every detail of this great work of art. The priestly service at the heavenly altar is performed by angels. The Lamb himself, as the High Priest, sacrifices his blood into the chalice that stands on the altar. A circle of angels, some with the instruments of torture of Golgotha in their hands, surround the heavenly ritual. In this painting (of which only the central motif of the Lamb of God is shown here) we recognise 'holy matter-of-factness'; a lofty content is represented with extraordinary precision and clarity.

Also Raphael's painting, *Disputation of the Holy Sacrament,* shows spiritual reality, while on earth the sacrament of bread and wine is celebrated saints, theologians, artists and priests are gathered around the altar. Their attention is mostly on the centre of the altar where the consecrated host is standing. Only a group of heretics at the extreme left turns demonstratively away from the altar. The other participants are all observing or thinking about what is taking place at the altar. Above the altar, borne by angel figures in clouds, are the great saints of the Old and New Testaments, who are still involved with what is happening on the earth. Above them

Figure 19. Van Eyck brothers, The Lamb of God, *completed 1432, now in St Bavo Cathedral in Ghent, Belgium.*

the Risen One with his wounds sits on a throne, and at his sides those who prepared humanity for his coming on earth, Mary and John the Baptist. At the top is the Father God surrounded by mighty angel figures.

In the composition of this painting we see three circles: the largest circle around Christ, a smaller circle around the dove, and the smallest circle formed by the host on the altar. In a certain sense there is one more circle of which we can only see the radiance, for from a point above the painting golden rays fall on the top part where the Father

Figure 20. Raphael, Disputation of the Holy Sacrament, *Vatican, Rome.*

is pictured. This composition creates the impression as if the ubiquity of the Father is condensed into the sun around the Christ, into the presence of the Spirit in the form of the dove, and, finally, into the tiny little host. In the transubstantiated bread heaven and earth come together, heaven and earth become one community.

When an offering is made on earth, the heavenly hosts are called to bring this offering to full reality. This is described in the offering of Manoah in the Old Testament. Manoah's wife, who was childless, entreated Yahweh for the birth of a child. Then 'a man of God' appeared who announced that she would bear a child who would be dedicated to God as a Nazirite. When she made a burnt offering together with her husband as directed by the stranger, he revealed himself in the flame: 'And when the flame went up toward heaven from the altar, the angel of the LORD ascended in the flame of the altar while Manoah and his wife looked on' (Judges 13:20). Only then did they recognise the stranger who had visited them. Only then did Manoah and his wife see and understand what happened.

Figure 21. Rembrandt, Sacrifice of Manoah. *1641, Gemäldegalerie Dresden, Germany.*

Rembrandt very subtly portrayed this story, in which a spiritual reality revealed itself in a ritual act. The angel is hardly visible as he ascends above the sacrificial fire. Without a doubt we may add to the Greek proverb, 'in the sacrificial smoke the gods descend to the earth', the words, 'in the sacrificial smoke the gods ascend to heaven'. Thus the elements of fire and smoke become mediators between heavenly and earthly creatures.

Prayer and offering

Prayer is also something which draws spiritual reality that is greater and more encompassing than a single individual can bring about. A fresco in South Tyrol, Italy pictures the 'prayer mantles' of Mary and Christ. Under these mantles the faithful are assembled, protected by the intercession of Christ and Mary. In a fiery circle above the praying community the Father is shown, who shoots arrows to the earth. The arrows are flung back off the mantle of Christ. Some art historians view this as a symbolic indication of an epidemic of the plague. In the Middle Ages people prayed during such calamities to Christ, Mary and the archangel Raphael, to avert the disease. This fresco reflects how people imagined this.

The motif of intercessory prayer, however, is much older. In a mosaic from around the year 530 in Ravenna, Italy we see Christ praying in Gethsemane before his disciples. What is pictured here is the prayer of the community of disciples, fortified by the intercession of Christ.

A touchingly primitive relief depicts an individual praying who is taken up in the embrace of an angel. The praying human being is pictured with spiritual realism in the mantle of a praying angel. In our prayer the angel can accomplish his heavenly task on earth and shine upon the human being.

The three great examples of offerings in antiquity are pictured in a famous mosaic in the church of Sant Apollinare in Classe in Ravenna, Italy. At one altar, Abel (with a lamb), Melchizedek (with bread and wine) and Abraham (with Isaac) all make their offerings. The presence of the Godhead is indicated with an eloquent gesture: the curtain of the spiritual world opens and the hand of God appears.

Finally, in Rembrandt's painting, *The Blessing of Jacob* (Figure 15, p. 105), the ritual act of blessing is represented more subtly and tentatively than in earlier times. It was a time when spiritual reality had to be expressed differently. Naturally, Rembrandt was an artist who had a unique ability to represent the spiritual in earthy reality. But he was also a child of his time – a time in which, more than ever before, the human being was thrown back onto themselves.

Anthroposophy speaks of the birth of the consciousness soul; human beings no longer felt themselves as natural parts of a greater whole, but became conscious of themselves as individuals.

In the gesture of the blessing Rembrandt portrayed a spiritual reality without the classical elements traditionally used in such scenes. Only the light, which streams out of Jacob's blessing hand, shines around his grandson Ephraim, and is strongest around the heart, still expresses a spiritual reality. From Rembrandt's time on,

Figure 22. Madonna and Christ with prayer mantles. c. 1400, St Proculus, Naturno, South Tyrol, Italy.

Figure 23. Christ praying in Gethsemane, c. 530, San Apollinare Nuovo, Ravenna.

Figure 24. Praying angel. Jerpoint, Ireland.

Figure 25. The Offering of Abel, Melchizedek and Abraham, Sant Apollinare in Classe, Ravenna.

human beings have to experience this reality in themselves. We can no longer depend on forces we are allowed to receive only from outside or above for our blessings, but we must build the spiritual power to hand these on as gifts to others. That is what Rembrandt seemed to show in this great painting.

After Rembrandt the connection with physical reality developed more and more in western art, until with the beginning of abstraction 'the spiritual in art' – to use Kandinsky's phrase – began to speak again. Perhaps this development, which is as far from ended, will offer potential in the future to bring the separate worlds of ritual, art and culture into mutual interplay again.

12

The Unborn and the Dead in Ritual

When I gave a course about ritual as I was writing this book, the impression rose in me that no matter how deeply we penetrate into this realm, time and again we come to a point where we are facing an enigma. This has to do with the area where the visible ritual changes into a spiritual reality. The borderline between these two realms is not absolute; there is a 'twilight zone' where we can observe with different senses, albeit semi-consciously or supra-consciously.

In a number of ritual forms we find indications of the spiritual reality that lives behind this borderline. Not only God and human beings, but also the unborn and the dead, adversary powers, hierarchies, and the Trinity are all addressed and receive a place in the rituals. In the confusing multiplicity of invisible worlds and beings there is, however, one centre point, which is at the same time the ultimate objective of every form of religion: the sacrament is primarily a service for God. There are some forms of liturgy that make it seem as if God and human beings are the only ones who exist. But when we look beyond these exceptions we find that in most cultures the unborn, the dead, the hierarchies and adversary powers have a place in the sacrament.

Ancestor worship, which plays an important role in 'primitive' cultures, is probably the oldest form of ritual. Also in early Christianity the dead are still important mediators between humanity and God.

The way toward birth

If we are familiar with pre-existence, it is not difficult to imagine that the unborn on their way to the earth, also want to connect with the sacrament. This is implicit in the annunciation of the birth of John the Baptist to his father Zechariah.

In this annunciation the archangel Gabriel made known who John actually was, months before he was to be born. Both Zechariah and his wife Elisabeth belonged to a lineage of priests. Although their behaviour was blameless, God had not blessed them with the birth of a child. When one day it fell to old Zechariah by lot to make the offering, he brought the scented offering in the sanctuary of the temple, while the people in the forecourt accompanied the offering with prayer. These two elements, the scented offering within, and the prayer of the people without, together formed the offering as a whole. Then an awesome angel figure appeared to the right of the altar.[1] This archangel, who made himself known to Zechariah as Gabriel, announced to him the birth of a son. He mentioned several characteristics of this child. John is 'predestined' to fulfil a great task as the preparer for the Messiah:

> But the Angel said to him: 'Do not be afraid, Zechariah, for
> your prayer has been heard; your wife Elisabeth will bear you
> a son, and you shall call him John. You will be filled with joy
> and gladness; many will rejoice because of his birth. Great
> will he be in the sight of the Lord. He will drink no wine nor
> anything intoxicating, and even from his mother's womb will
> he be filled with the Holy Spirit. He will turn many sons of
> the people of God to the Lord their God again. He will be his
> forerunner and will pave his way, bearing within him the spirit
> and the power of Elijah, to change men's hearts so that fathers
> shall rediscover the meaning of childhood, and those who
> have become alienated from God shall find the meaning of the
> Good again. So shall he make a well-prepared people ready for
> the Lord.' (Luke 1:13–17).

If we try to imagine where the unborn child was while the archangel announced his birth, it is not difficult to realise that he was present at that moment. Long before birth, the unborn soul is already directing its attention to its future parents, which is something small children in our time are sometimes spontaneously able to speak about. From another perspective, the unborn soul is still in the womb of the hierarchies.

There is a tradition in Germany that the unborn soul has to

wait nine months with its physical birth so as to be able to make its journey through the nine hierarchies. During that period the future child receives its task for its earth life. In the sacrament of Baptism in the Christian Community this is expressed in the words, 'This soul sent down from the community of spirit to that of earth.' The soul of a newly born child is no accidental product; in the community of the spirit before birth it has received a mission that has to be realised in the earthly community. How what is pre-ordained in this way relates to earthly reality is a whole chapter by itself – not to mention anything about the person's own will and ideas.

The continuation of the pre-birth path of John shows that there exists in the world of the unborn a complete consciousness, both of the world of the earthly and of unborn fellow travellers. Thus Luke described how in the encounter between Mary and Elisabeth the unborn participate in earthly reality: 'And when Elisabeth heard the greeting of Mary, the babe leaped in her womb' (Luke 1:41). The unborn recognised his future fellow traveller.

It is not difficult to imagine that the unborn, who are able to see, and see through, things with different eyes than human beings living on earth, are 'interested' (the word is too mundane, but I cannot find a better expression) in genuine ritual on earth. For they participate in the heavenly ritual between the midnight hour and conception, as they prepare for their future incarnation.[2] The unborn carry these images in themselves while, with a strong longing, they direct their attention to the earth. What would it mean for them when the parents, who are expecting their future child, participate in an sacrament?

A mother had the following dream, even before she was aware of the fact that she was going to have a child:

> I dreamt that my husband and I were invited to a special
> festivity. My friend was called by a voice to pray for all
> invited guests and for the child she was expecting. (She was
> expecting her first daughter and was in her fourth month.)
> Thereafter I was also called to say a prayer, because I was also
> expecting a child. I wanted to concentrate and reflect but
> found no words, no matter how I tried. I felt very unhappy.
> Then I noticed that the ceiling of the room was moving up
> and dissolving. I stood alone next to the baptismal font of

the church. Many people were sitting in the pews before me. Desperately I kept trying to find words. Then from above inexpressibly beautiful colours streamed down. Exquisitely beautiful music started sounding and grew to a terrific thunder, from which a voice took form. Hearing the words that were so mightily spoken we were frightened and fell down on the ground facing the earth. Then sounded the words: 'He comes from my heart. I am well pleased with him. He returns to my heart.' Then I woke up.

Here the annunciation of the child in the dream is part of a liturgy for which no words can be found. Not only did words fail, but the woman who was dreaming this was also unable to express what sort of colours there were, what kind of music, what sounds she was hearing there. She was overwhelmed by the grandness of the sacred incident which, literally and figuratively, took place above her head. In these images, colours, sounds and words something was revealed of the unborn child, whom she was already carrying unconsciously.

It is well-known that mothers who are expecting a child, sometimes have irresistible cravings. Most of the time these are not things to pay much attention to, but sometimes they give some indication of the character of the coming child. Gretchen Schulze, the wife of Heinrich Ogilvie, one of the founders of the Christian Community, had the capacity to perceive her children in their own nature long before they were born. Ogilvie wrote in his autobiography:

In 1929 we had our fourth child, a son. My wife recognised him again as the little boy who, three years earlier, had introduced himself to her with the words, 'I am Michael.' This had happened when, while in a deep sleep, she became consciously clairvoyant. She told me this three years before his birth.[3]

With three of her four children Gretchen had impressions and cravings during her pregnancy:

Before her son Friedrich was born she dreamt that she was given a tour of a great cathedral. During the pregnancy she felt a strong need to participate regularly in the Act of Consecration of Man. The child later became a priest.

While she expected her second child she dreamt that the unborn led her into her own body and showed her the wonders of the physical body and its organs. This child, Helmut, later became a physician. It was as if the dream wanted to tell her that before his birth he was already working on his later life task.

Of the third child, Sonja, I cannot remember how her mother met her before her birth.

The last one was Michael. During her pregnancy Gretchen wanted to see theatre performances. Evening after evening she was sitting in the balcony in the theatre watching plays. Michael later became an actor.

In cases like this it is impossible to separate what comes from the mother and what comes from the child. But I can quite imagine that in the reciprocal relationship between mother and unborn child such intuitions, dreams and actions may grow.

Another experience that a mother told me indicates that, conversely, the child also receives impressions from the mother, long before it is born. One of the members of our congregation told me that during her pregnancy she practised a piano piece by Bach for weeks. When the child was born she did not touch the piano for a long time. Only when the child was already able to speak did she go back to the same composition by Bach. The little girl perked up her ears and said with great conviction that she had known that piece for a long time.

By analogy with such reports, which mothers nowadays can frequently tell, we may well imagine that attending an sacrament in the time before birth is not only significant for the parents, but also for the coming child. It is not only a form of 'pre-birth education', but the child is also able to recognise what the significance is of the life of Christ, and his place on earth. 'Like recognises like'. This saying can only become reality if we offer our unborn souls impressions they can indeed recognise!

The dead

It seems as if the unborn have been manifesting themselves more clearly only since the last decades of the twentieth century.[4] Experiences with the dead, however, have been frequent for a long time. In many cultures we see that the dead form part of ritual acts. I will here limit myself to Christianity.

The New Testament describes in picture language how the dead work into ritual, both on earth and in heaven. For instance, the Letter to the Hebrews speaks of 'a cloud of witnesses [that] surrounds us' (Heb.12:1). The previous passage tells us who are meant: 'They all became witnesses to the Spirit through faith, although they did not themselves experience the fulfilment of the promise' (Heb.11:39). It was not only the first Christians who were martyred for their faith, but the author of the Letter to the Hebrews also mentions the old prophets, including Isaiah, 'They were stoned, they were sawn in two, they were killed with the sword' (Heb.11:37 RSV). Isaiah fled his persecutors and hid in a hollow tree. King Manasseh had the tree sawn in two with Isaiah in it.[5]

All these souls of the dead, Christians as well as saints and prophets from Old Testament times, belong to the cloud of witnesses who are indispensable for the celebration of the sacrament. The witnesses (the Greek word for witnesses is *martyres,* the source of our word martyrs) who died for their faith celebrate together with the hierarchies the heavenly liturgy in the spiritual world.

In the previous chapter I discussed the liturgy that is celebrated by the angels (represented in the painting *The Lamb of God* by the Van Eyck brothers). The Book of Revelation, however, also speaks of souls of the dead who perform a priestly task at the heavenly altar. It describes the hundred and forty-four thousand servants of God who carry a seal on their foreheads, standing 'before the throne and the Lamb, clad in white garments' (Rev.7:9). The text speaks here of *stole leuke,* white priestly robes with the stole, the sign of priestly dignity. The dead are sometimes similarly pictured in illuminated manuscript such as the eleventh-century Bamberg Apocalypse.[6]

That this passage of Revelation is about the heavenly ritual does not become clear in most translations, such as 'they serve him day and night in his temple' (Rev.7:15), The Greek word *latreuousi* means literally 'to bring ritual', while for 'temple' the word *naos* is used, the Holy of Holies. 'The dead offer the ritual to God in his Holy of Holies' could be the translation. The white robe, the priestly garment, came into being because on earth they had 'washed their garments and made them white with the blood of the Lamb'

(Rev.7:14). The soul went through catharsis by the trials it had undergone on earth.

The next chapter of Revelation relates in picture language how earthly and heavenly ritual are woven together and reinforce each other. The ritual act of the scented offering has its origin in the heavenly ritual, but the offerings and prayers of the living on earth strengthen this heavenly offering:

> And another angel came and stood at the altar with a golden censer; and he was given much incense to offer with the prayers of all those who are devoted to the Spirit, on the golden altar in the sight of the throne. And the smoke of the incense rose up with the prayers of those who are devoted to the Spirit, from the hand of the angel before the countenance of God. (Rev.8:3f).

From the earthly ritual prayers and offerings rise up to heaven. The angels use this spiritual substance, enrich it with their power, and bring this offering to God – an imagination of the weaving together of the earthly and heavenly ritual, in which the dead perform an important, mediating function.

The picture of this upward movement of the offering is completed with a downward movement:

> Then the angel took the censer, filled it with the fire of the altar and scattered it over the earth. Then thunder pealed, voices sounded, lightning flashed and the earth shook.
>
> And the seven angels who had the seven trumpets made ready to trumpet. (Rev.8:5f)

What is offered on earth and in heaven is 'raw material' for the further development of creation. God can use it to continue his creation. With our naive consciousness we usually imagine that development is identical with growth and progress. But life repeatedly shows that development also includes decline, destruction and involution.

When I asked one of my very old friends shortly before his death how he was doing, he said, 'In satisfactory decline.' We could also say that of earth evolution as a whole: for further perfection, a 'dying earth existence' (a formula from the Christian Community Creed) is eventually necessary. We see in the course of the Book of Revelation also that this metamorphosed offering substance of the living, the dead and the hierarchies triggers destructive forces on earth, in order to make possible the progress of the world as it ultimately leads to the New Jerusalem.

What sounds in the Apocalypse in radical angel language, sounds in the Act of Consecration of Man in human terms in the prayer, 'In the offering be born the fire of love, creative of being.' Love creates a being, physical, psychic, or spiritual. Out of this offering-flame 'timeless existence' can be awakened, a future creation consisting of the good that is willed and carried out on earth. Thus our offerings become building stones of the New Jerusalem, the future spiritualised creation of which the Book of Revelation speaks.

The interaction between the living and the dead

In the catacombs, in the early days of Christianity in Rome, we can see an example of the reciprocal action of the living and the dead in the ritual. Every altar was both a tomb and an offering table where the dead could participate in the holy meal. Every person who died in Christ became a co-celebrant of the sacrament. Above the altars too, the presence of the dead was indicated by countless pictures of *orantes,* figures representing the dead in the classic attitude of prayer with raised hands. Frequently under the fresco is the name of the person who died with the well-known text, *ora pro nobis,* pray for us.

Those who have died in Christ are the best helpers with ritual acts. Their spiritual power – and through them the resurrection power of Christ – can flow into the ritual act. I have already quoted a crucial formulation Rudolf Steiner used to demonstrate what occurs in a ritual act: 'Sense-perceptible actions are performed, and spirit streams into the actions.'[7] These words speak of processes, activity and movement: where sense-perceptible processes take place, the spiritual (the dead, the hierarchies, the Trinity) can stream in.

These classic pictures and concepts also give material to recognise what is in the Act of Consecration of Man. There the dead also have an indispensable role. They pray and offer together with us. Every Act of Consecration is also a service for and with the dead. At the beginning of the Offertory this is explicitly articulated with the words, 'With me may there bring it all who have died.' Everyone who has died can participate in the sacrament.

The next part of the Act of Consecration, the Transubstantiation, speaks of the dead who have 'brought Christ to life within them,' with the entreaty that their prayer mantle may envelop us, 'Their sheltering power ray forth to us.' In the corresponding passage of the Latin mass the great saints are invoked with the entreaty for protection and assistance. The Act of Consecration of Man in this place engages all who during their lives took Christ into themselves and brought him to life. These are not just the well-known saints, but also the countless 'sainted ones'.

From my own experience I will describe here how these two passages from the Act of Consecration can speak to us more concretely. When we want to accompany the dead not just for a few days or weeks, but through the years, the anniversaries of their passing are important mileposts. It is no accident that in early Christianity the death day was called *dies natalis,* day of birth (into the spiritual world).

As a priest I accompany many people who have died, so I direct my attention to one of them in particular around the anniversary of their death. The previous evening I call up an image of the person as vividly as I can from my memory. In this image, which is permeated with memories, affection and empathy, I let my love stream to him or her:

> May my love be interwoven
> As my heart's offering
> In the sheaths that now surround you,
> Cooling all your heat,
> Warming all your cold.
> Live – love-upborne,
> Light-rayed-through – on upward.[8]

Then I invite the person to be present at the Act of Consecration of Man the next day. That day I call up the images once more before the sacrament begins, and give them a place in the celebration – or co-celebration – of the service. You can even include the dead when receiving communion. As a matter of fact, especially in that moment of the Act of Consecration, if we give them a place, they can be nearer to us than ever.

To my surprise, in the course of years I have discovered that it is also possible to develop a relationship with people who have died whom I had not known in life. For instance, I studied the biography of Walter Gradenwitz, who was one of the founders of the Christian Community. I became interested in him through stories of members in my congregation who had experienced him as a priest. They described him as someone who was aware of karmic relationships between people and, out of that insight, was able to reconcile differences between people. He could handle difficult situations of destiny objectively. He knew the world of the unborn and the dead from his own experience. Heinrich Ogilvie said of him, 'It was evident that the portal of death had been open to him all his life, and that the portal of birth had never closed.'

During the time when I was occupied with this person whom I had not known when he was alive, pictures of his life and his personality became very clear and recognisable. Eventually I was able to experience his presence at the altar – in the congregation where he had himself been the priest – in our joint celebration of the Act of Consecration of Man. He was now working from the other side, to inspire the living.

In one of his poems we can clearly feel how strongly he himself lived with the dead at the altar:

Mass for the Dead

When you all, silently, enter my soul
That has expanded into your world,
And listen to the words my soul is praying,
Illumined by the consecration's light –
When I then lift the round disc of the bread
And raise the chalice rim up to my mouth
So that crystalline clarity may spread
Throughout the body and the soul may live
Within the draught of health's pure love:

I feel, not I alone am here receiving
Sustenance that opens up wellsprings of grace –
You also bow, and a long line of souls
Departed, both dear and barely known,
Passes through me.
Earth's barriers have fallen away –
As messenger I was allowed
To lead you to His flock.

Whoever has the eyes to see, or the sense organ to feel, will perceive the countless numbers of the dead who assemble together with the living at the altar to have communion with Christ. In this poem Walter Gradenwitz described that a long line of the dead, familiar ones but also some he hardly knew, passed through him when he received communion. When we invite the soul of one particular person who has died to the altar it is a well-known phenomenon that after some time he brings his companions with him. The dead form communities of souls who are familiar to each other. In the world of the dead this phenomenon is even more prevalent than in the world of the living.

Walter Gradenwitz prepared during his life on earth what he wanted to do between death and rebirth. This was a fully conscious preparation, of which the following poem, which he wrote shortly before his death, is testimony:

Light of Soul

Perhaps the hour very soon will sound
When I no longer may be near my companions
Of shared endeavours, here in earthly life –
Then may memory, deeply engraved
Into the panorama of the life I led
Strengthen me for yet more ardent union
So I may direct my being to the quiet deeds
That faithful they fulfil in service of the Christ,
And, raying love, bless all their earnest striving.
If thus from death spring forth the spirit's seeds,
Soul-light can permeate the earthly night,
The light in which we meet the Coming One.

In the last sentence of the poem it becomes evident that the connection between the living and the dead is not the purpose of the sacrament. But by the connection of the living with the dead, and the dead with the living, the encounter with Christ, in whose name we assemble at the altar, can come about.

Sometimes the presence of the dead clothes itself in images that arise in us, sometimes also in words. From my diary, in which I record such experiences, I will now quote two brief events that illustrate this:

On 24 November, 2006 it was exactly 20 years ago that M.v.G. died. I thought of her several times that day, as also in the service the next day. During the words spoken over the bread and wine, I suddenly saw in front of me the room of the Last Supper. I recognised it not only from a journey to Israel, but also from a photograph M.v.G. had given me years before. And with that clear picture of the room of the Last Supper her love and her warmth streamed to the altar. Thus the dead work in us, through us. The link was a small gift that was handed to me in deep affection during life.

27 October, 2007, the anniversary of K.v.d.L.'s death. The evening before I thought of her briefly and made a mental note to commemorate her in the Act of Consecration of Man. The next day, as I was taking communion during the service, the following words suddenly sounded in me: 'Lord, I am not worthy to have you enter my house; speak only a word, then my servant will be healed.' Only then did I remember that these were the words K.v.d.L. always spoke after I had brought her the communion in the last phase of her life. The words had vanished from my memory. Quite unexpectedly, as if prepared by my thoughts of the dead person, an aspect of her essential being, which this person wanted to share during her life, emerged again. In this way the dead are connected with us.

I have tried to express this strong connection with the dead, and their call on us, in the following poem:

The silence reverberates in my ears,
The dead sound forth –
Too great to put in words.
In unknown tongues
They sing to us,
They look us in the eye.
O let me hear
What they with mortals
Wish to share.
Although I walk my way alone,
We are with many.

A stronger feeling of community is not possible. What we can accomplish to some extent with companions in earthly life, becomes infinitely stronger and deeper between the living and the dead. In the Act of Consecration of Man lies the potential of community with the dead in Christ's name.

13

Hierarchies and Adversary Powers

The artist Joseph Beuys once made the intriguing statement, 'In the twentieth century the mysteries are taking place at the train station.'[1] Perhaps we could say the same of airport terminals. What he meant was that in every place where people meet each other to welcome or say goodbye, mystery and initiation can take place. But this statement does not take the world of the hierarchies and adversary powers into account. These do not limit themselves to train stations or airports. On the contrary, they look for any place where love or hate, freedom or captivity, truth or lies, respect or contempt reign. We might imagine that an angel feels at home (pardon the trite expression) in a consecrated space, just as the angel of a congregation connects himself with a particular group of people in a consecrated space.

The one-sidedness of views such as that of Beuys leads to the fact that in certain movements the baby is thrown out with the bathwater. For instance, I once read in an interview the assertion that Christ does not belong to a church. That sounds just as intolerant as saying that Christ can only be found in this one single place. That is sectarianism. As soon as we start thinking in terms of exclusivity, we close the door to part of outside reality – and we even close the door to Christ.

What we can do is to speak of gradations of 'presence'. A spiritual atmosphere may be superficial or concentrated, serene or stirring. For the founders of the Christian Community, Rudolf Steiner once indicated what is evoked in the mass:

> The mass can just as well be an offering to the devil as an offering to God. It is not the insignificant thing Protestant consciousness would like to make it. The mass ... is never the nothing that the Protestants would like to make it.[2]

At the altar, in the Eucharist, we serve either God or the opposing powers. That sounds very different than the assertion that the being of Christ is not part of a church. Some people are still able to imagine that we serve God at the altar – but the devil? To understand this we have to familiarise ourselves with the concepts of white, grey and black magic. When a sacramental act is performed at the altar we invoke, through it, positive or negative spiritual powers. In that way we enter into the little explored realm of magic.

What does the celebration of a ritual bring about? Around the time of the foundation of the Christian Community, Rudolf Steiner gave a series of public lectures. In these he touched on the essential difference between ritual acts and daily acts; and in these lectures it also became clear that ritual creates something of real essence.

> When the cult [ritual] can once again be truly understood,
> those who possess this understanding will be able to make
> clear to their pupils that enactments in sacred cults and rites
> have an immeasurably greater significance for the cosmos
> than deeds performed by men in the external world with
> mechanical tools and the like. Tools, as you know, also
> play a part in cult and ritual. When true ceremonial, true
> ritualistic enactments are again established in place of what is
> customary today, initiates will be able to say to their pupils:
> An enactment in cult or rite is a call to the spiritual powers of
> the universe who through the deeds of men should be able to
> unite themselves with the earth.[3]

The ritual words and acts, which have been given by the initiate from the heavenly ritual, has the capacity to invoke spiritual beings. Elsewhere Steiner gave several examples of invocation:

> When we do this or that we are continually peopling the
> astral plane. If we think these thoughts through clearly, we
> have the meaning of church ritual: that is, not to make use of
> any kind of substances on the physical plane, except such as
> have meaning, whereby meaningful beings arise on the astral
> plane. When for instance one kindles the smoke of incense

one does something which has purpose; one burns a particular substance and creates beings of a particular kind. When one passes a sword through the air in four directions one creates a definite kind of being.

It is the same with the priest, when he makes definite movements with his hands, to accompany definite sounds o, i, u, intensified by repetition: *Dominus vobiscum.* The sound is regular, the air is brought into definite vibrations intensified by definite movements of the hand, and a sylph [an airy elemental being] is called into existence.[4]

In this passage it becomes clear that ritual acts create something real. We might also speak of magical acts when spiritual beings are invoked. But here we have to distinguish three different realms: white, grey and black magic.

The distinguishing characteristic of white magic is that it is a form of thinking, speaking and acting that is connected with love, freedom and selflessness. We could even say: the more selfless it is, the more efficacious the magical act is. We can say the same about the working of prayer. The more selflessly a prayer is thought, prayed and spoken, the more powerful will it be. Magic works through the media of ritual, prayer and meditation. The purpose of white magic is the perfection and spiritualisation of the earth. Not until the new creation, which the New Testament calls the New Jerusalem, is this goal fully achieved.

The future spiritualised creation is filled with the divine. In our current, earthly world, however, we have to create special, consecrated spaces – in ancient times these were the mystery places – to make the manifestation of the divine possible. The spiritual world can create an oasis of peace in temples, churches, places of silence, meditation rooms, mosques and synagogues – as long as reverence, attention and mutual respect reign in these places. Even more so, whoever is able to see behind the outer form of the ritual will discover the angel of the congregation.

This is described in the following fragment from the book by Dagny Wegener about clairvoyant perceptions with which she was blessed all her life:

When on Sunday morning people participate in a worship service, become inwardly quiet, listen to the organ and to the priest who reads the Gospel, a mood of reverence may grow. That is an atmosphere the spiritual world loves. Thus it happened one Sunday that suddenly a spiritual being appeared, that was at first like a shadow. I could not quite make it out. Later this shadow-like being came more often. I did not ask what it could be, because I had already learned that the spiritual world does not like curious people and immediately withdraws from them.

Then in Holy Week two years ago, I saw that the same figure I had seen a number of times was an angel. Suddenly he stood like a radiant figure beside the altar. He stayed there only for a moment. Then he hovered quickly and lightly, the arms crossed over the chest, in front of the first row and looked the first person who sat there full of goodness in the eye. Then he went to the next person. With this wondrous expression in the eyes he hovered from one person to the next and looked everyone of them in the eye. In retrospect I realised that it can hardly have been more than three seconds, but it is possible to observe a person in a short time.

Then I had to think: but this is the angel of the congregation! No one else would be able to do this in the same way. And suddenly it was clear to me that this angel observed each of us individually. When he came to the second row, where I was sitting, I felt his eyes directly on my face. I can only say that it was a profoundly moving impression to sense, to know: this is the angel of the congregation who participates in us, as we also participate in this worship service.

I am certain that in every church, of whatever denomination, where there is a mood of reverence, where the Gospels are really read, where politics are kept out and only what is Christian streams in, there is also an angel of the congregation who looks the people in the eye, hoping also to be observed by them.[5]

Black magic

In opposition to the many forms of white magic, which have the power to evoke certain elemental beings (such as the sylph described by Rudolf Steiner on p. 202) and hierarchies (such as the angel of the congregation experienced by Dagny Wegener), we have black magic which is able to evoke demonic elementals and hierarchies. Just as freedom, love and selflessness characterise white magic, unfreedom, hatred and egoism characterise black magic. And as the purpose of white magic is to serve God, so black magic aims to worship and serve adversary powers.

Opposite the striving of white magic to spiritualise the earth (the New Jerusalem) stands that of black magic to turn the earth into 'Babylon'. The name Babylon is used in the Book of Revelation (Chapter 17) to denote the part of humanity that has made itself into slaves of matter. Just as the Heavenly Jerusalem descends from heaven to the earth, so is Babylon the city that is built upward to attack heaven from below and bring about the triumph of the physical world.

One of the characteristics of black magic is that all the elements of the sacrament are used to evoke evil. Thus in the Church of Satan there are priests of Satan who celebrate masses. Just as in the consecration of a lay person as priest in a Christian church, in the Church of Satan a lay person is consecrated by a black magician after extensive preparation.

Although the adversary powers have grown considerably in our world, and seem have the whole earth in their grip, the Book of Revelation says about this power: 'The beast that you see was there once; now it is not; but it will rise anew out of the abyss, and then it will meet its destruction' (Rev.17:8). The fact that this power of evil, with all its overwhelming force, is in the end powerless when faced with the good, was described in an impressive way by an 'expert through experience' in black and white magic, Ulla von Bernus. For years she was a priestess of Satan and making propaganda for black magic in the German media – but from one day to the next she moved from black magic to white magic. In an extensive interview she said:

I had a spiritual encounter with a person I knew, who had died. I had the following experience. We went together through a dark passage; I was in front, he behind me. Eventually the dark passage opened out into a square, but everything remained shrouded in dimness as in the twilight when day turns into night. We stood there and looked into the dim light. Suddenly it was raining grains of wheat. Endless quantities of wheat rained from heaven. And then the experience of Golgotha came very distinctly. Not the three crosses, but only Christ on the cross. And Christ spoke with a loud voice: 'In the end I will nevertheless be the victor.'[6]

Here we see that without any display of power the adversary power is in the end powerless in the face of the good. This experience led Ulla von Bernus to white magic. Since then she has been acting publicly, not only to describe from her own experience that black magic is a dead-end road, but also to sound the strongest possible warnings against grey magic, which today is practised in a wide variety of forms. In the media, in all kinds of occult and semi-occult movements, in science, art and religion, in countless forms of addiction, grey magic has been forcing its way into our cultural life today. The remedy Ulla von Bernus described in her interview for protection against these influences is interesting: 'Knowing about these things is the most important factor.'

While the opposing powers hide behind many different masks, the strongest weapon in the fight against these powers is insight. These powers are dangerous as long as we don't know, or don't want to know about them. They work in semi-conscious and unconscious realms. *The Sleep of Reason Produces Monsters* is the title of an etching by the Spanish artist Goya. It shows a human being who fell asleep sitting at a table. Above and around him an army of demons and animal figures come together.

Against this background – the tactics of the adversary powers and the weapon of consciousness – the call of Christ, 'Watch and pray' or 'Keep awake and pray' (Matt.26:41) is more critically apposite than previously imagined. Watchfulness to see through the workings of evil, prayer to the highest leader who has already overcome evil out of his inner being – these are two weapons that give us the strength

Figure 26. Francisco Goya, The Sleep of Reason Produces Monsters, *etching, c. 1799.*

to stand our ground in the battle. Before the New Jerusalem becomes reality there is a long road we have to travel where, just looking from the outside, it does not appear that we can achieve much against the overwhelming power of evil.

At the lowest point of this road, evil even becomes so strong that not just ordinary people, but also the saints are injured and killed by it.

> And it [the beast] was given the power to unleash a war against those human beings who were devoted to the spirit, and to defeat them. All-embracing power was given to it over all tribes and peoples and languages and races. (Rev.13:7).

The only weapon that stands up against this destruction is endurance or patience. *Hypomenein,* literally 'to remain under it, to hold out,' is the redeeming word in this most disturbing chapter of Apocalypse: 'Here only the power of endurance and the faith of those who are devoted to the Spirit will stand the test' (Rev.13:10). In other words, not only is it impossible to eradicate evil, that is not even the point. Only at the end of earth evolution do the ways of good and evil definitively part. Before that time, weeds will have to grow up together with the fruits of development.

Heavenly hierarchies

In all circumstances, ritual is a means for calling up spiritual powers, both the good and the bad. The fact that at the altar the priestly service of the hierarchies can also be evoked is illustrated by the following event, which made a deep impression in the Middle Ages.

In the year 1022 Henry II, Holy Roman Emperor, visited the Michael Sanctuary of Monte Gargano in Italy. In the cave where the archangel once revealed himself he attended the mass. It was said that no one was allowed to be in that space at night, because Michael himself then celebrated the heavenly liturgy at the altar with his angels. The archangel had once said to Lorenzo, one of the saints who lived there, 'At night I myself, the Lord of this holy place, will celebrate the mass.' In spite of the warning, the pious emperor had himself locked into the cave that night.

In the night Michael appeared with his host of angels and performed the sacrament. But when he took the eternal Gospel (see Rev.14:6) and handed it to the Emperor, the latter trembled in fear. Thereupon Michael spoke, 'Fear not, you are chosen by God. Take this sign of heavenly peace and joy.' And he touched the emperor's hip. The latter survived this overwhelming experience, but ever afterwards he walked with a limp. The story reminds us of Jacob and his encounter with the angel who struck him on his hip, so that he limped (Gen.32:22–32).

The nocturnal encounter of Henry II demonstrates that the sacrament of human beings on earth is but a pale shadow of the overwhelming ritual of the 'sons of God'. As Dionysius the Areopagite said in one of his writings, God clothes himself in 'holy mantles'. These mantles mitigate the unbearably blinding light of the Godhead in order to allow human beings to see it. Conversely, it is the task of human beings to climb the ladder of the hierarchies step by step, in order eventually to become one with the Godhead. Dionysius called this process 'deification', becoming God.

The hierarchies celebrate continuously in 'holy vestments of light'. Psalm 29 describes that the *bnei elim,* 'sons of the gods', perform the ritual to the Lord in 'holy vestments of light' ('heavenly beings ... worship the Lord in holy array' rsv). In Psalm 96:8f, which also sings of the heavenly ritual, we read almost the same words, but with one important difference. Here the term of the 'holy vestments of light' which may remind us of the white priestly vestment, is not used for angels but for human beings. 'Worship the LORD in holy array,' says the rsv. That a form of ritual is again referred to is clear from the previous sentence: 'Ascribe to the Lord the glory due his name; bring an offering, and come into his courts!'

Pictorially we might say: whereas purified human beings may bring offerings in the forecourt of the divine temple, the angels celebrate the heavenly liturgy in the sanctuary. In the Holy of Holies, however, stands the High Priest of humanity, Christ, and offers himself for us.

Celebrating at an altar on earth is the beginning of a 'golden chain', an *aurea catena,* as the alchemists used to call the mysterious connection between heaven and earth. Every hierarchy on Jacob's ladder is an indispensable link in this golden chain. Human beings make it possible for this golden chain also to touch the earth. For without human beings the chain would be broken – and the earth with its kingdoms of nature would remain unredeemed.

To conclude this chapter, a detailed description follows by someone who spontaneously saw in the Act of Consecration of Man what takes place in the world of the hierarchies while an sacrament is celebrated on earth.

Right after the beginning of the Act of Consecration of Man on Sunday, 16 March, 1986, I 'saw' that the whole event was being observed by a large host of angels. They formed a dome as it were over the altar, the priest and the congregation, and looked down on us with very relaxed, peaceful and at the same time concentrated (but not fixed) attention. They were countless in number because their forms blended into each other here and there; they were rather like various intensities of light. They did not stand in any 'arrangement' but formed an 'orderly chaos' that gave the impression of great harmony and beauty (like the natural beauty of clouds in the sky). The whole atmosphere, the forms and most of all the manner in which they looked at us reminded me strongly of certain paintings by Leonardo da Vinci.

As the service progressed the separate forms dissolved into patterns that continually changed in colour and form, pastel-like shades, soft, yet intense. Now and then openings formed in this ceiling of moving colours, or rather passages, especially in the vicinity of the altar. These were actually formed by the bodies of angel beings; their bearing then expressed total devotion, creating (literally and figuratively) an passage to the heavens. In this passage there was light of a most remarkable quality which is difficult to express in the right words; maybe: very friendly, inviting, benevolent. It also had a different composition than earthly light. It gave the impression of harmony and joy, not so much ecstatic joy, but more a joy filled with gratitude, attention, peace and love.

This was my spontaneous experience which simply arose without prior intention.

The way the writer formulated this illustrates how difficult it is to put into words a spiritual experience that is constantly changing as it occurs. For our perception we witness perfect harmony between above and below, between spirit and body, between receiving and giving. The description reminded me of the end of a verse that young children in Waldorf Schools speak daily. These two final lines are a summary of the entire principle of prayer, verse and ritual:

> From you come light and strength,
> To you rise love and thanks.

These words express the alpha and omega – the origin and goal – of ritual: when human beings begin to realise what they have received from the Godhead, something begins to flow back to God. Our visible and invisible worlds are filled with light and forces. And we, citizens of earth and inhabitants of heaven, sons of man and sons of God, owe him love and thanks. What streams back from us, out of our own initiative, is new for the divine world. The imagery of the psalms has an expression for this: a 'new song'. Psalm 96 that describes the priestly function of the human being, begins with the words, 'O sing to the LORD a new song.' With our prayers, with our offerings, that are kindled in the tough reality of earthly existence, we bring to the Godhead something that had not been created before. In the new song, creation finds its progress and future. That is the purpose of the sacred act on earth.

14

The Future of Ritual

Watch over your thoughts,
Soon they become words.
Watch over your words,
Soon they become deeds.
Watch over your deeds,
Soon they become habits.
Watch over you habits,
Soon they become character.
Watch over your character,
Soon it becomes destiny.

This anonymous poem illustrates how step by step we ourselves, to an important extent, determine our own future. It begins with the thoughts we think. It is well-known that thoughts sooner or later take root, begin to lead a life of their own, and turn into reality. Everything we think, speak and do sooner or later creates something real.

We can also apply the message of this poem to liturgical thinking, speaking and acting. Everything we think, speak and do at the altar creates a reality that has significance not only for the here and now, but also for the future.

In different pictures and words St Paul expressed this in his well-known hymn to love: 'Now we still see everything in dark outlines, as in a mirror. Some day we will see everything face to face.' (1Cor.13:12). What happens with our love at the altar has, to a certain extent, the character of something in dark outlines. We have already seen that the full reality of our offerings, our prayers, thoughts and ritual acts is enacted in the spiritual world. Not the living, but the dead see face to face. That applies especially to ritual.

Rudolf Steiner showed these two 'faces' of ritual very concretely in a lecture in which he described the funeral service of the Christian Community:

> Let us suppose, my dear friends, that here we have a mirror and here again some object. You see the reflection of the object in the mirror. You have the two things – the original and the reflection. Similarly when a ritual for the dead is enacted, there are the two things. The ritual enacted by the priest before the coffin is a reflection. It is a reflection, and it would be no reality if it were not a reflection. What does it reflect? The acts of the priest as he stands before the dead body have their prototype in the supersensible world. For while we celebrate the earthly rite before the physical body, and the etheric body is still present, on the other side the *heavenly* ritual is enacted by the Beings beyond the threshold of earthly existence. Over yonder, the soul and spirit are received by what we may call a ritual of welcome, just as here on earth we are assembled before the dead for a ritual of farewell. A cult or ceremony is only true when it has its origin in reality.
>
> ... If we celebrate a true ritual for the dead, a supersensible ritual is enacted simultaneously. The two work together. And if there is sanctity, truth and dignity in the prayers for the dead, beings of the hierarchies in the supersensible world echo in the prayers for the dead and weave into them. The spiritual world and the physical unite.[1]

Particularly through our offerings do we create something for the future. In a certain sense, no future is possible without sacrifice or offerings. That already holds true for daily life. If parents are not willing to make sacrifices for their children as they are growing up, they will miss opportunities and possibilities for the future. This is not only a necessity for the children; for the spiritual world offerings are building stones for the future creation. This also comes to expression in the final sentence of the Offertory in the Act of Consecration of Man: the offering begets timeless existence. By making offerings human beings justify themselves in the spiritual world; they become recognised entities.

Although this timeless existence is the ultimate goal and perspective of our ritual acts and offerings, we all know perfectly well that the road to this goal is full of pitfalls. Before the power of white magic can come to manifestation and the good is firmly planted on earth, the power of evil has to take centre stage, undisguised. We can read this in countless apocalyptic prophecies. The prophet Daniel was among the first to foresee this spectre of the future. In a vision he saw a future in which God was to be deprived of the daily offering. In lieu of this offering, 'the abomination that makes desolate is set up' (Dan.12:11). What does this strange picture mean? Usually a historical event is then referred to that took place in the year 168 BC, when King Antiochus Epiphanes (176–164 BC) erected his own statue in the Holy of Holies of the Jewish temple after he had conquered Jerusalem. Christ himself mentioned this prophecy on the Mount of Olives when he said:

> Then, when you see the aberration of the human self set up,
> a hideous form [the abomination that makes desolate], where
> it should not be (let the reader penetrate what he reads with
> his thinking), let all those who are in Judea seek refuge in the
> mountain heights (Mark 13:14).

The Greek expression used here gives us a clue: *to bdelygma eremōseōs,* the spectre of separation, loneliness. In the word *eremōseōs* we recognise our word 'hermit'. The ego inflates itself, usurps the place of God and lets all forms of community fall apart like loose sand. The first time this happened was when Antiochus Epiphanes erected his statue in the Holy of Holies, as if he wanted to say, 'I am God.' In countless different ways the Roman Caesars imitated him. History repeats itself right into the present day.

But the ultimate spectre of desolation is the appearance of the Antichrist, prophesied by Daniel in this picture. Simultaneously, he already saw the Son of Man coming in the clouds. The apocalyptic grandeur and tragedy of the Second Coming sounds in the words Daniel hears the Son of Man speak, 'There is none who contends by my side against these except Michael, your prince' (Dan.10:21). These words conclude the image of the prophecy of Daniel where Christ stands on the far side, Michael on this side of the river that separates heaven and earth, but the bridge that connects both sides has yet to be built.

Christ's prophecy of the spectre of desolation was preceded by the prediction of the destruction of the temple. In his time, the idea of the demise of the temple was like the spectre of desolation of the world. This is how people felt when the temple of Ephesus burned down in 356 BC and when the Jewish temple was destroyed by the Romans in AD 70. As the little apocalypse on the Mount of Olives began with the picture of the destruction of the temple, it ended with the destruction of the physical world, 'Heaven and earth will pass away, but my words will not pass away (Mark 13:31).

The image of the spectre of desolation is more than the culmination of egoism and power display. It is also more than the current image of human beings who by their greed and recklessness destroy the earth and the seas and pollute the air. It is a picture that is 'set up where it should not be'. Christ calls on the reader to be conscious of the fact that this is the image of human beings who expel the Godhead and put themselves in his place – the image of the Antichrist.

Counter-ritual and Antichrist

Daniel did not use the name, and yet in his imagery we can recognise the working of the Antichrist: a beast, a he-goat inflates himself to such a size that he robs heaven of its stars and tramples upon them.

> It [the horn of the he-goat] magnified itself, even up to the
> Prince of the host of heaven; and the continual burnt offering
> was taken away from him, and the place of his Sanctuary was
> overthrown. And the host was given over to it together with
> the continual burnt offering through transgression; and the
> truth was cast down to the ground, and the horn acted and
> prospered. (Dan.8:11f).

Here the image of the counter-ritual arises, of the mystery of the Antichrist, as St Paul later called it. St Paul saw in his visions a similar picture. It is noteworthy that he continued and differentiated the imagery of Daniel in his Second Letter to the Thessalonians. We gain the impression that what Daniel saw in a still distant future had come nearer, had become more concrete for Paul. What would take place remained the 'mysteries of chaos', literally *a-nomia,* lawlessness, but in the projection in time Paul distinguished different phases:

> First there must come the great breach of faith, the separation from the world of Spirit; the man of chaos must be revealed, the son of perdition, the spirit of opposition who considers himself exalted over everything that is called divine and deserves reverence, and who ultimately puts himself in the place of God in the temple of God and poses as a god. Do you remember that I told you this repeatedly when I was still with you? Then also you know that a power still restrains him, until, when his time has come, he will appear openly. The mysteries of chaos are already working. If there were not a power which still restrains them, they would even now break out from the centre. In time, the magical destroyer will be revealed without disguise. But Jesus the Lord will sweep him aside with the breath of his mouth and destroy him by his coming in the Spirit [*epiphaneia*]. (2Thess.2:3–8)

Here we have a succinct summary in a 'little Apocalypse' of the whole drama of the Antichrist, his rise, display of power, and fall. Obviously, his activity is not the work of one sole being. The Antichrist receives his effective power from the adversary forces.

In the previous chapter we quoted Ulla von Bernus. She stood for years 'face to face' with these adversary forces until, by the appearance of the Crucified One, she received insight into the would-be power of evil. She described the actual situation before and behind the scenes as follows:

> At the moment, Satan has a solid grip on the earth, and many people are fascinated by him. Because the white side is giving him the possibility to work to a certain point, of course he does so. That is why at this time there are hardly any boundaries he has to observe. People notice that, and it is the reason why many imitate him with black and grey magic. From morning to night people are inundated by the media, and much of this comes from the black side. Most of what comes from the media is of a black or grey nature. This works

on in the unconscious of human beings. Today people are losing the practice of lucid thinking or keen concentration. In my courses I have also noticed that only few people are inclined to walk a true spiritual path. Most of them strive for grey practices. The moment I told my students that what is needed is a true spiritual path, I lost almost 90% of them because that is too uncomfortable for them. Satan is the lord of chaos. For this reason his work will end in a catastrophe. The white side will not prevent this. It will not intervene, for human will is free.[2]

In the words of a contemporary of ours, this is what Paul called the mystery of chaos. Because Ulla von Bernus also trains students, and views the world with different eyes, she sees how often, due to insufficient consciousness, people currently become the victims of grey and black magical practises.

We don't need to be prophets to see that Christianity will be put to some critical tests in the future. Everywhere we hear opinions and assertions that aim to stop everything that takes place at the altar. In the past we there were religious persecutions, clandestine churches, refugees of religious wars. In our time it is no longer just groups of people who fight each other for life or death, it is not one sole person who acts as the Antichrist, but anti-Christian activity mostly occurs *en masse* and anonymously. It is a sobering perspective that, viewed from the outside, Christianity seems to be a lost cause. The Apocalypse admits of no doubt that this will be a future stage of Christianity.

In the previous chapter we discussed the passage where we are told that to the beast that rises from the sea it will be given (by whom?) 'power to unleash a war against those human beings who were devoted to the spirit, and to defeat them. All-embracing power was given to it over all tribes and peoples and languages and races.' (Rev.13:7). Apparently, there is an even higher power than the beast, someone who orders time, and determines when the power of the adversary reaches its culmination, and when his power comes to an end. The counter-ritual is personified in its most perverse guise in the image of the whore of Babylon:

The woman was clad in purple and scarlet garments, and she
was brilliantly adorned with gold and precious stones and
pearls. In her hand she held a golden cup full of hideous and
impure Beings, the offspring of her unchastity ... And I saw
the woman drunk with the blood of those who are devoted
to the Spirit, and with the blood of the martyrs of Jesus.
(Rev.17:4,6).

The rites of the adversary powers make use of a spectre of cup and
communion: the Christians are fought, tortured and killed in order to
drink their blood. Black magic has a predilection for such ways. Black
magic is all about consciously tormenting and killing living beings:

White magicians would give to other souls the spiritual life
they carry within. Black magicians have an urge to kill, to
create a void that surrounds them in the astral world, because
a void gives them a field in which their egoistic desires may
play. They need the power they gain by taking the vital force
of everything that lives – that is, by killing it. This is why the
first sentence on the tables of black magic is: Life must be
conquered.[3]

The heavenly temple

As the counter-ritual of the opposing powers evokes a world of
destruction, so the Godhead, by the ritual in God's temple, calls the
future creation into being. The temple in heaven appears – 'and the
ark of his covenant was seen' (Rev.11:19 RSV). One could say: the
inner being of God comes to manifestation. The ark of the covenant,
which was carried through the desert by the Jewish people, contained
three ritual objects that meant a promise for the future: the stone
tablets with the law of Moses, the green staff of Aaron, and the golden
vessel with manna, the heavenly bread. In the imagery of the Old
Testament the stone tablets express the physical body that in future
can be transformed into 'spirit man'. The physical (mineral) world
is then spiritualised. The green staff of Aaron indicates the world of
life forces, which will be spiritualised into 'life spirit', Finally, manna

is the expression of the soul forces, which will be transformed into 'spirit self'.[4]

When the ark of the covenant becomes visible in heaven, the future human being will be revealed in the inner being of the Godhead. This exceptional perspective of the future is reflected in the Act of Consecration of Man in the epistle for the Advent season, where it speaks of 'man's becoming, in which God's becoming lies hidden.'

Also the end of the Book of Revelation, which describes the end of earth evolution, is clothed in a ritual image. The New Jerusalem appears as 'the dwelling of God among men' (Rev.21:3). The Greek has the word *skēnē,* which means 'tent' or 'tabernacle'. What was the tent of God? The tabernacle was the place where God lived on earth, as long as the people of Israel worshipped the Godhead and made offerings to him there. Later this function was taken over by the temple of Solomon. In the prologue to the Gospel of St John the word *skēnē* appears in the passage, 'And the Word became flesh and lived [literally: 'tabernacled'] among us' (John 1:14).

As he once, during his life on earth, lived among us, so in a distant future will God's dwelling place envelop us forever. The future image of the tabernacle appears in Revelation 7 when John heard that God would stretch his tent over his people. There is a subtle difference here with the image of Chapter 21:

And he who sits upon the throne will shelter them [Greek: 'spread his tent over them'] (Rev.7:15).

See the dwelling of God among men! He will dwell in their midst, and they shall be his people [Greek: Behold, the tabernacle of God among the people, and he will 'tabernacle' among them] (Rev.21:3).

The abyss between God and man is closed. In Daniel's imagery, the bridge across the great river is built. John uses radically new words: 'They will see his countenance' (Rev.22:4). At one time, while still separated from God, people said, 'He who sees God dies.' As we are now, we cannot bear the sight. We may perhaps see a reflection, a shadow, darkly, as in a mirror. But when part of humanity becomes spiritualised in the future, these individuals will behold God face to face. In the New Jerusalem the duality between earthly and heavenly ritual will be lifted. By their deification, human beings will be able to participate in the heavenly liturgy. This is the reason why the Apocalypse describes that there will be no temple in the city. Here on earth a city without a temple is an abomination, not only for the people, but undoubtedly also for the spiritual world. In the New Jerusalem there will be no temple, for 'the Lord, the divine Ruler of all, is himself its temple together with the Lamb' (Rev.21:22).

Until now it might appear as if only those who confess Christ will be able to find the way to this future creation. But the Apocalypse adds: 'All spiritual treasures [*timai,* tributes] of the peoples [*ethnōn*] and all achievements of soul shall be brought into this city' (Rev.21:26). Only now it becomes evident that there are 'many ways to Rome', that there are also legitimate ways that lead to the New Jerusalem. Implicitly this was already revealed in the imagery of the Apocalypse: there is not one gate, but twelve gates that give access to the city.

New forms of community

In order to experience at least something of the future ritual today, we need the help of the dead at the altar. It seems to me that this offers great future potential for the altar sacrament. Can we develop means to celebrate the sacrament together with the dead? The sacrament cannot be carried by a single person, but needs a community to carry it. This obviously begins with a visible congregation on earth, but it can develop into a community with the dead and, through the dead, into a community with the hierarchies and the Trinity.

In the Book of Revelation the dead play a special role. They are mentioned for the first time as souls *(psychai)* under the altar (Rev.6:9). At this stage of evolution they are still powerless. They suffer from the after-effects of their persecution and martyrdom on earth: 'How long will you delay your judgment upon those who live on the earth' (Rev.6:10). In this lamentation sounds the impatience of the all-too-human view which is not yet capable of recognising decisive moments. Here the dead receive the white garment, and the instruction to rest and wait until their number is full.

Hereafter the dead appear in a variety of guises: as the great assembly in white garments before the throne (Rev.7:9), as those who sang and played their harps before the throne (Rev.14:2f), as riders on white horses (Rev.19:14), and finally as kings and priests of Christ (Rev.20:6). Here again souls are mentioned. Only now does their true part in the Apocalypse come to manifestation. In the same way, we may anticipate that in the future their protective power will become ever stronger for those who unite with the dead in prayer and ritual.

The power of the sacrament lies in the community. The priest celebrates out of the I if he worthily performs the service. This I, however, has to act supra-personally out of the forces of the community. Rudolf Steiner once characterised this future growth of community – which can grow into sacramental deeds not only in the sacraments, but also in the priesthood of all the faithful – as follows:

> Association means the possibility for a higher being to express itself through the members when they are united. This principle is general for all life. Five people together, who think and feel harmoniously together, are more than 1 plus 1 plus 1 plus 1 plus 1; they are not just the sum of the five, just as our body is not the sum of the five senses. Men's living together, and within one another, has the same significance as the living together of the cells within the human body. A new, higher being is in the midst of the five – yes, even among the two or three. 'Where two or three are gathered together in my name, I shall be in their midst.' It is not the one, or the other, or the third, but something entirely new that springs from the union. The new entity arises only when the one lives in the other, when the single individual person draws strength not only from himself, but also from the others. But that can happen only if each lives selflessly in the other. Thus, human associations are the secret places where higher spiritual beings descend in order to work through the single individuals, just as the soul works through the members of the body. ...
>
> Therefore, spiritual science does not speak in abstractions when it speaks of a folk-spirit, or folk-soul, or the spirit of some other community. One cannot see the spirit who works through an association, but he is there; and he is there through

the brotherly love of the people working in the association.
Just as the body has a soul, so a guild or brotherhood has a
soul; this is not just a figure of speech.

People who work together in a brotherhood are magicians,
because they draw higher beings into their circle. One no
longer has to call to witness the machinations of spiritism
when one works out of brotherly love in a community. Higher
beings do manifest themselves there. When we give ourselves
over to brotherhood, this giving, this merging in the totality,
is a steeling, a strengthening of our organs. When we then act
or speak as members of such a community, it is not the single
soul that acts or speaks in us, but the spirit of the community.
This will be the secret of the progress of mankind in the
future: to work through communities.[5]

The New Jerusalem, the future creation, is the outcome of such
forms of community. Twelve roads lead to the twelve gates of the
city. Twelve angels stand on the gates. The names of the twelve tribes
of Israel are written on the gates of the city, while the community
of the twelve apostles forms the foundation of the walls. What the
Book Revelation wishes to say with this imagery is that with twelve
the circle of community is complete. St Augustine called the number
twelve the symbol of community.

In the Christian Community the sacrament begins with the words,
'Let us worthily fulfill the Act of Consecration of Man.' That is not
the 'royal we', where the priest speaks royally for himself. The word
'us' gives space to all who assemble at the altar – visible and invisible,
near and far, living and dead, human beings and angels, all who look
up to Christ and wish to serve him.

This principle is valid for every form of community, in which the
individual may come to himself in order to come to the other. Such
communities form part of the twelve roads that lead to the twelve
gates. The New Jerusalem owes its existence to single individuals who
put a strong I in service of him who wishes to dwell in their midst:

When each of us
Was thrown back onto himself
I grew slowly

As a clear crystal
In the chasm of loneliness.
Now can we finally
Come together again
In crystal clear variety.
A new heaven
Stretches above us.
On the table is space
For bread and wine.
One in diversity
We shall more than ever
Be together.

Bastiaan Baan

Notes

Introduction

1 Faivre, *Access to Western Esotericism.*
2 An expression of Dionysius the Areopagite, author of a teaching about hierarchies.
3 In the Latin mass the text is: *Sanctus, sanctus, sanctus Dominus Deus Sabaoth. Pleni sunt coeli et terra gloriae tuae.* The original text in Isaiah is: 'Holy, holy, holy, Lord of hosts; the fullness of the whole earth is his glory.'

1. Forms of Worship in the Stone Age

1 I have elaborated on this subject in my book *Old and New Mysteries,* Chapter 4, 'The Egyptian Mysteries'.
2 Mees, Allard W., 'Der Sternenhimmel von Magdalenenberg. Das Fürstengrab bei Villingen-Schwenningen: ein Kalenderwerk der Hallstattzeit.' *Jahrbuch Römisch-Germanisches Zentralmuseum* 54, Mainz 2007, pp. 217–64.
3 Steiner, *Initiation Science,* lecture of Sep 9, 1923.
4 Steiner, *The Four Seasons and the Archangels,* lecture of Oct 12, 1923.
5 Steiner, *From Mammoths to Mediums,* lecture of Sep 10, 1923, p. 268.
6 Steiner, *From Mammoths to Mediums,* lecture of Sep 10, 1923, p. 280.

2. Nature Religion and Ancestor Worship

1 This description is a free rendition of Rudolf Frieling's comments on Psalm 104 in his *Hidden Treasures in the Psalms.*
2 Steiner, *Anthroposophical Leading Thoughts,* No. 112, p. 85.
3 Lagerlöf, *Karln.*
4 Steiner, *Good and Evil Spirits,* lecture of May 13, 1908, p. 115.
5 Steiner, *Verses and Meditations,* p. 207.
6 Neihardt, *Black Elk Speaks,* Chapter 3, 'The Great Vision'.

3. The Patriarchs in the Old Testament

1 See Frieling, 'Trees, Wells and Stones' in *Old Testament Studies.*

4. Jewish Ritual and the Temple of Solomon

1 Bock, *Moses,* p. 52.

2 Agrippa von Nettesheim, *Magische Werke,* p. 269; translated by P.M. from the Dutch translation of the German.

3 Steiner, *Mythen und Sagen,* lecture of Dec 28, 1907, pp. 230f.

4 Frieling, *Old Testament Studies.*

5 Bock, *Kings and Prophets,* p. 149.

6 Steiner, *Architecture as a Synthesis of the Arts,* lecture of Dec 12, 1911.

7 Holladay, *The Psalms through Three Thousand Years,* pp. 168, 175, 180f.

8 We find similar words in the Act of Consecration of Man during the censing of the Offering.

9 See Teichmann, *Der Mensch und sein Tempel: Megalithkultur in Irland, England und der Bretagne,* pp. 208f.

10 Adonis is the symbol of plant growth. In Byblos (Lebanon) annual festivals were celebrated in remembrance of the death and resurrection of Adonis.

11 Marie Steiner's poem 'Isola San Giulio' in Wiesberger, *Marie Steiner-von Sivers: Ein Leben für die Anthroposophie,* p. 488. The original German is:

> Nicht bist du frommen Betern zu vergleichen,
> Die still dahingewandert, erdenfremd:
> In Flammen schuf dein Geist, der Welten läutert
> Und sie emporhebt aus der Niederung Schmach.

12 Wiesberger, *Marie Steiner: Briefe und Dokumente.*

13 Wiesberger, *Rudolf Steiners esoterische Lehrtätigkeit,* p. 266.

14 Steiner, *The Temple Legend,* lecture of Oct 23, 1905 (morning), footnote 5, p. 378.

5. Mithraism

1 Bemmelen, *Zarathustra,* pp. 62f.

2 One of the most famous Mithraea is in Monte Gargano, Italy. After the Mithraic religion had been eradicated, this became the most famous Michael sanctuary of the Middle Ages. Worshippers from across Europe would go to Monte Gargano on Sep 29 to celebrate the Michael festival. See Baan, *Old and New Mysteries,* Chapter 3.

3 Steiner, *Building Stones,* lecture of April 24, 1917, pp. 255, 257f.

4 Rudolf Steiner, *Inner Reading and Inner Hearing,* lecture of Dec 26, 1914, p. 154.

5 Steiner, *Building Stones,* lecture of May 1, 1917, p. 279.

6. The Origin of the Christian Ritual

1 The gospel writers used remarkable expressions to indicate this transformation, Matthew (17:2) used the word *metamorphōthē* (akin to our word metamorphosis). All evangelists spoke of the *doxa* (glory, majesty, manifestation) of his being. Rudolf Frieling used *Wesens-Erstrahlung* (radiance of the true being) to translate *doxa.* See the chapter on the Transfiguration in his *New Testament Studies.*

2 Jerome, *De viris illustribus,* 2.

3 Bock, *Caesars and Apostles,* Chapter 9, p. 290.

4 Augustine, *En Evangelium Ioannis Tractatus,* 15.8.

5 There is no stenographic record of this lecture. Mathilde Scholl's notes were published in *Beitrage zur Rudolf Steiner Gesamtausgabe,* No. 110, Easter 1993.

6 Steiner, *Building Stones,* lecture of April 24, 1917, p. 262.

7 Steiner, *The Sun Mystery,* lecture of April 13, 1922, p. 93.

8 Steiner, *The Mysteries of the East and of Christianity,* lecture of Feb 3, 1913, p. 16.

9 Apuleius, *Metamorphoses,* 11.23.7.

10 Clement of Alexandria, *Protrepticus,* 12.120.1f.

11 Clement of Alexandria, *Protrepticus,* 11.112.12.

12 Cyril of Jerusalem, Ambrose, John Chrysostom and Theodore of Mopsuestia gave such catechisms.

13 Rinn & Jüngst, *Kirchengeschichtliches Lesebuch,* p. 9.

14 See Schermann, *Studien zur Geschichte und Kultur des Altertums,* Vol. 6, p. 186.

15 Emmerich, *The Visions,* (12th Station, 7) Vol. 3, pp. 78f.

16 Emmerich, *The Visions,* (12th Station, 7–8) Vol. 3, pp. 79f.

17 Frieling, *The Eucharist.*

7. The Development of the Eucharist

1 Pirim, the founder of the monastery of Reichenau, Germany, connected the name of an apostle to each of the twelve sentences. See Müller and Suckau, *Werdestufen des christliches Bekenntnisses,* pp. 41f.

2 Hegesippus, *Memoires,* quoted in Eusebius, *Church History.*

3 Ignatius, *Letter to the Ephesians,* 20.

4 Cyprian, Epistle 53, in Roberts, Donaldson & Coxe, *Ante-Nicene Fathers,* Vol. 5.

8. Christianity and Renewal

1 Eusebius, *Church History,* Book 2, Ch. 25.

2 Steiner, *Christianity as Mystical Fact,* pp. 137f.

3 Steiner, *Good and Evil Spirits,* lecture of June 1, 1908, pp. 151f.

4 See, for instance, Hillerdal & Gustafsson, *We Experienced Christ,* and Schroeder: *Von der Wiederkunft Christi heute.*

5 Stöckli, *Wege zur Christus-Erfahrung,* Vol. 3, p. 261.

6 See Schroeder, *Vom Erleben der Menschenweihehandlung,* pp. 165f.

9. The Sacrament of Bread and Wine

1 Quoted from Selawry, *Johannes von Kronstadt,* pp. 71f.

2 Quoted from Rudolf Frieling, *Messe-Studien,* p. 40 (unpublished undated paper).

3 From *Beiträge zur Rudolf Steiner Gesamtausgabe,* No. 30, Easter 1993.

10. The Senses in the Sacrament

1 I describe this in more detail in my book, *Ways into Christian Meditation*.
2 Steiner, *How to Know Higher Worlds*, p. 23.
3 Sydow, *Aus der Begründungszeit der Christengemeinschaft*, pp. 55f.
4 Steiner, *Broken Vessels*, lecture of Sep 8, 1924, p. 23.
5 Nestle, *Sprachlicher Schlüssel zum griechischen Testament*.
6 *Die Christengemeinschaft* (journal) 1976, p. 55.
7 Steiner, *Agriculture*, lecture of June 16, 1924.
8 Steiner, *Natur- und Geistwesen*, lecture of Feb 11, 1908, p. 207.
9 Frieling, *Die Feier*.
10 Steiner, *Truth-Wrought-Words*, p. 91.
11 Bossis, *He and I*, diary entry of April 25, 1939.
12 Steiner, *Esoteric Lessons*, lecture of Dec 5, 1909, p. 462.
13 Steiner, *Die menschliche Seele in ihrem Zusammenhang*, lecture of April 13, 1923, p. 164.
14 Lusseyran, *And There Was Light*, p. 221.
15 Ritchie, *Return from Tomorrow*, pp. 48f.
16 Emmichoven, *The Reality in Which We Live*, p. 7.

11. Ritual and Visual Art

1 The name Cabeiri is related to the Hebrew word *kabir*, meaning 'great, mighty'; the word 'kobold' may also have the same root. See Ehrhardt, *Samothrake*, p. 101.
2 J.W. Goethe, *Faust*, Part 2, Act 2, p. 122.
3 Steiner, *Goethe's Faust in the Light of Anthroposophy*, lecture of Jan 17, 1919, p. 202.
4 There are a number of brief passages about Jesus in Josephus, mainly in *Antiquities of the Jews*, as well as in *The Jewish Wars*, though scholars are divided about their authenticity.
5 Clement of Alexandria, *Paedagogus*, III, 33.
6 Steiner, *The Festivals and their Meaning*, lecture of March 27, 1921, p. 170.
7 Perre, *Van Eyck. Das Lamm Gottes*.

12. The Unborn and the Dead in Ritual

1 The description in Luke's Gospel of this appearance has led to a remarkable formula in the Latin mass. In the Offertory the archangel Michael is mentioned *stantis a dextris altaris incensi*, 'standing on the right of the altar of incense.'
2 Steiner, *The Inner Nature of Man*, lecture of April 13, 1923, pp. 92–94.
3 Ogilvie, *Jakob, wo bist du?*
4 Bauer, Hoffmeister & Goerg, *Children who Communicate Before They Are Born*.
5 Talmud, *Yevamot 49b*. Source: Wikipedia.
6 Harnischfeger, *Die Bamberger Apokalypse*, Fig. 14.

7 Steiner, *Broken Vessels,* lecture of Sep 8, 1924, p. 23.
8 Steiner, *Truth-Wrought-Words,* p. 91.

13. Hierarchies and Adversary Powers

1 Interview with Peter Brügge, *Der Spiegel,* June 4, 1984 *(www.spiegel.de/spiegel/print/d-13508033.html).*
2 Steiner, *Vorträge bei der Begründung der Christengemeinschaft,* lecture of Sep 7, 1922, pp. 47f.
3 Steiner, *Supersensible Influences in the History of Mankind,* lecture of Sep 29, 1922, p. 47.
4 Steiner, *Foundations of Esotericism,* lecture of Oct 30, 1905, pp. 219f.
5 Wegener, *Blick in eine andere Welt.*
6 Weirauch & Bernus, *Schwarze und weisse Magie.*

14. The Future of Ritual

1 Steiner, *Karmic Relationships,* Vol. II, lecture of June 27, 1924, p. 237.
2 Wegener, *Blick in eine andere Welt.*
3 Steiner, *An Esoteric Cosmology,* lecture of June 2, 1906, p. 48.
4 See Steiner, *Theosophy,* p. 55.
5 Steiner, *Brotherhood and the Struggle for Existence,* lecture of Nov 23, 1905, p. 9.

Bibliography

Agrippa von Nettesheim, *Die Magische Werke,* Wiesbaden 1997.

Baan, Bastiaan, *Lord of the Elements,* Floris Books, UK 2015.

—, *Old and New Mysteries,* Floris Books, UK 2014.

—, *Ways into Christian Meditation,* Floris Books, UK 2015.

Bauer, D., M. Hoffmeister, H. Goerg, *Children who Communicate Before They Are Born,* Temple Lodge Publishing, UK 2005.

Bemmelen, D.J. van, *Zarathustra,* Stuttgart 1975.

Bock, Emil, *Caesars and Apostles,* Floris Books, UK 1998.

—, *Das Evangelium,* Stuttgart 1984.

—, *Kings and Prophets,* Floris Books, UK 2006.

—, *Moses: From the Mysteries of Egypt to the Judges of Israel,* Floris Books, UK 1986.

Bossis, Gabrielle, *He and I,* Pauline Books & Media, USA 2013.

Casel, Odo, *Das Gedächtnis des Herrn in der altchristlichen Liturgie,* Freiburg 1918.

Catechism of the Catholic Church, Libreria Editrice Vaticana 1994.

Edusei, Kofi, *Für uns ist Religion die Erde, worauf wir leben,* Stuttgart 1985.

Ehrhardt, Hartmut, *Samothrake,* Stuttgart 1985.

Emmerich, Anne Catharine, *The Visions of Anne Catherine Emmerich,* 3 vols, Angelico Press, USA 2015.

Emmichoven, F.W. Zeylmans van, *The Reality in which We Live,* New Knowledge Books 1964.

Faivre, A. *Access to Western Esotericism,* Albany 1994.

Frieling, Rudolf, *The Eucharist,* Floris Books, UK 1999.

—, *Die Feier,* Verlag der Christengemeinschaft, Stuttgart 1928.

—, *Hidden Treasures in the Psalms,* Floris Books, UK 2015.

—, *New Testament Studies,* Floris Books, UK 1994.

—, *Old Testament Studies,* Floris Books, UK 1987.

Goethe, J.W. *Faust,* tr. by Bayard Taylor, Random House 1950.

Harnischfeger, Ernst, *Die Bamberger Apokalypse,* Stuttgart 1981.

Hillerdal, Gunnar, & Berndt Gustafsson, *We Experienced Christ,* Temple Lodge Publishing, UK 2016.

Holladay, W.L. *The Psalms through Three Thousand Years,* Minneapolis 1993.

Kirk, Robert, *The Secret Commonwealth of Elves, Fauns and Fairies,* London 1893; reprinted New York 2007 with an introduction by Marina Warner.

Lagerlöf, Selma, *Karln,* Modernista, Stockholm 2017.

Lusseyran, Jacques, *And There Was Light,* Floris Books, UK 1985.

Manen, Hans Peter van, *Das vierte Geheimnis,* Dornach 1997.

Müller, Adolf, & Arnold Suckau, *Werdestufen des christliches Bekenntnisses,* Stuttgart 1974.

Neihardt, John G. *Black Elk Speaks,* University of Nebraska Press 2000.

Nestle, D. Eberhard, *Sprachlicher Schlüssel zum griechischen Testament,* Giessen 1977.

Ogilvie, Heinrich A.P. *Jakob, wo bist du? Lebensbericht,* privately published 1982.

Perre, Harold van de, *Van Eyck. Das Lamm Gottes. Das Geheimnis Schönheit,* Tielt 1996.

Rinn & Jüngst, *Kirchengeschichtliches Lesebuch,* Tübingen 1915.

Ritchie, George, *Return from Tomorrow,* Revell Books, USA 1978.

Roberts, Alexander & James Donaldson & A. Cleveland Coxe (eds.) *Ante-Nicene Fathers,* Christian Literature Publishing, Buffalo, N.Y: 1886 (revised by Kevin Knight at *www.newadvent.org/fathers/050653.htm*).

Schermann, Theodor, *Studien zur Geschichte und Kultur des Altertums.*

Schroeder, Hans-Werner, *Mensch und Engel,* Stuttgart 1979.

—, *Vom Erleben der Menschenweihehandlung,* Stuttgart 1997.

—, *Von der Wiederkunft Christi heute: Verheissung und Erfüllung,* Stuttgart 1991.

Selawry, Alla, *Johannes von Kronstadt: Starez Russlands,* Basle 1981.

Steiner, Rudolf. Volume Nos refer to the Collected Works (CW), or to the German Gesamtausgabe (GA).

—, *Agriculture* (CW 327) Biodynamic Association, USA 1993.

—, *Anthroposophical Leading Thoughts* (CW 26) Rudolf Steiner Press, UK 1973.

—, *Architecture as a Synthesis of the Arts* (CW 286) Rudolf Steiner Press, UK 1999.

—, *Broken Vessels* (CW 318) SteinerBooks, USA 2002.

—, *Brotherhood and the Struggle for Existence,* Mercury Press, USA 1980.

—, *Building Stones for an Understanding of the Mystery of Golgotha* (CW 175) Rudolf Steiner Press, UK 2015.

—, *Christianity as Mystical Fact* (CW 8) Anthroposophical Press, USA 1997.

—, *An Esoteric Cosmology* (CW 94) SteinerBooks, USA 2008.

—, *Esoteric Lessons 1904–1909* (CW 266-1) SteinerBooks, USA 2006.

—, *The Festivals and their Meaning: Easter,* Rudolf Steiner Press, UK 1996.

—, *Foundations of Esotericism* (CW 93a) Rudolf Steiner Press, UK 1983.

—, *The Four Seasons and the Archangels* (CW 229) Rudolf Steiner Press, UK 1996.

—, *From Mammoths to Mediums* (CW 350) Rudolf Steiner Press, UK 2000.

—, *Goethe's Faust in the Light of Anthroposophy* (CW 273) SteinerBooks, USA 2016.

—, *Good and Evil Spirits* (CW 102) Rudolf Steiner Press, UK 2014.

—, *How to Know Higher Worlds* (CW 10) Anthroposophical Press, USA 1994.

—, *Inner Reading and Inner Hearing* (CW 156) SteinerBooks, USA 2008.

—, *Initiation Science and the Development of the Human Mind* (CW 228) Rudolf Steiner Press, UK 2017.

—, *The Inner Nature of Man and Our Life between Death and Rebirth* (CW 153) Rudolf Steiner Press, UK 2013.

—, *Karmic Relationships,* Vol. II (CW 236) Rudolf Steiner Press, UK 2015.

—, *Die menschliche Seele in ihrem Zusammenhang mit göttlich-geistigen Individualitäten: Die verinnerlichumg der Jahresfeste* (GA 224) Rudolf Steiner Verlag, Dornach 1992.

—, *The Mysteries of the East and of Christianity* (CW 144) Rudolf Steiner Press 1972.

—, *Mythen und Sagen. Okkulte Zeichen und Symbole* (GA 101) Rudolf Steiner Verlag, Dornach 1992.

—, *Natur- und Geistwesen. Ihr Wirken in unserer sichtbaren Welt* (GA 98) Rudolf Steiner Verlag, Dornach 1996.

—, *The Sun Mystery and the Mystery of Death and Resurrection* (CW 211) SteinerBooks 2006.

—, *Supersensible Influences in the History of Mankind* (CW 216) Rudolf Steiner Publishing Co. 1956.

—, *Theosophy* (CW 9) Anthroposophic Press, USA 1994.

—, *The Temple Legend* (CW 93) Rudolf Steiner Press, UK 2000.

—, *Truth-Wrought-Words,* SteinerBooks, USA 2010.

—, *Verses and Meditations,* Rudolf Steiner Press 2004.

—, *Vorträge bei der Begründung der Christengemeinschaft* (CW 344) Rudolf Steiner Verlag, Dornach 1994.

Stöckli, Thomas, *Wege zur Christus-Erfahrung. Das ätherische Christus-Wirken,* Dornach 1992.

Sydow, Joachim, *Aus der Begründungszeit der Christengemeinschaft,* Basel 1972.

Teichmann, Frank, *Der Mensch und sein Tempel: Megalithkultur in Irland, England und der Bretagne,* Stuttgart 1999.

Wegener, Dagny, *Blick in eine andere Welt: Begegnungen mit Verstorbenen und geistigen Wesen,* Stuttgart 1997.

Weirauch, Wolfgang, & Ulla von Bernus, *Schwarze und weisse Magie: Von Satan zu Christus,* Flensburger Hefte.

Wiesberger, Hella (ed.) *Marie Steiner-von Sivers: Briefe und Dokumente,* privately published, Dornach 1981.

—, *Marie Steiner-von Sivers: Ein Leben für die Anthroposophie,* Dornach 1988.

—, *Rudolf Steiners esoterische Lehrtätigkeit,* Dornach 1977.

Index

Biblical index

The Chymical Wedding of Christian Rosenkreutz
A Commentary on a Christian Path of Initiation

Bastiaan Baan

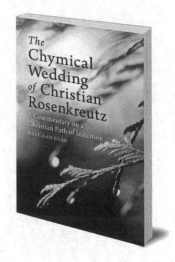

Containing the complete text of *The Chymical Wedding*, this timeless book explores the inner transformation of the soul. Baan's insightful interpretation and commentary makes this work accessible to modern readers. He uncovers the original significance, combining images and concepts from alchemy with insights from Rudolf Steiner's teachings.

florisbooks.co.uk

Sources of Christianity
Peter, Paul and John

Bastiaan Baan, Christine Gruwez,
and John van Schaik

'The three authors combine academic thoroughness with a
lively capacity to enter imaginatively into their theme.'
– *Camphill Correspondence*

This fascinating book paints a vivid picture of the three
apostles, exploring their similarities as well as their significant
differences, and demonstrating their continuing relevance
today. Beginning with a discussion of the pre-Christian
context, the authors conclude by tracing the esoteric streams
of Petrine, Pauline and Johannine Christianity in the first
few centuries after Christ. Crucially, they demonstrate
how all three apostles are equally essential in order to truly
approach the reality of Jesus Christ.

florisbooks.co.uk

Lord of the Elements
Interweaving Christianity and Nature

Bastiaan Baan

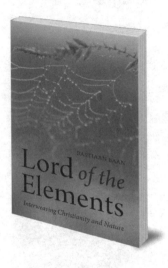

'This book can enable us to take a positive step towards
our right destiny as human beings. It can be used
as a friendly guide and source of encouragement.'
– *Perspectives*

In this unique work on the links between Christianity and
the natural world Bastiaan Baan explores the four classical
elements of earth, water, air and fire. Baan brings these elements
together with ideas from Rudolf Steiner's anthroposophy. He
also focuses on how elemental beings relate to the four elements,
and explores their role in our world.

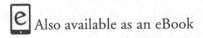 Also available as an eBook

florisbooks.co.uk

Old and New Mysteries
From Trials to Initiation

Bastiaan Baan

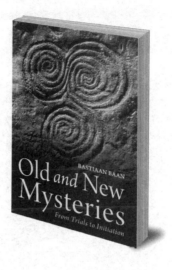

'Rich in references, rich in illustrations,
rich in knowledge and practical advice.'
– *New View*

This fascinating book compares and contrasts the trials
and rites that historically took place in the mystery centres
of antiquity with the modern-day experience of initiation.
Baan suggests that life itself, rather than a 'hierophant',
or guide, tests us and that this can lead to deeper spiritual
experiences between Christianity and the natural world.

florisbooks.co.uk